THE EVOLVING MAN

LIFE VIRTUES MEN DON'T TALK ABOUT

MARKHAM F. ROLLINS III

THE EVOLVING MAN
LIFE VIRTUES MEN DON'T TALK ABOUT
Copyright © 2024 by Markham F. Rollins III

All rights reserved. No part of this publication may be reproduced, stored in a retrieval system, or transmitted in any form or by any means, electronic, mechanical, photocopying, recording, or otherwise, without written permission of the publisher or author, except for the use of brief quotations in a book review.

Although the author and publisher have made every effort to ensure that the information in this book was correct at press time, the author and publisher do not assume and hereby disclaim any liability to any party for any loss, damage, or disruption caused by errors or omissions, whether such errors or omissions result from negligence, accident, or any other cause.

Adherence to all applicable laws and regulations, including international, federal, state and local governing professional licensing, business practices, advertising, and all other aspects of doing business in the US, Canada or any other jurisdiction is the sole responsibility of the reader and consumer.

Neither the author nor the publisher assumes any responsibility or liability whatsoever on behalf of the consumer or reader of this material. Any perceived slight of any individual or organization is purely unintentional.

The resources in this book are provided for informational purposes only and should not be used to replace the specialized training and professional judgment of a health care or mental health care professional.

Neither the author nor the publisher can be held responsible for the use of the information provided within this book. Please always consult a trained professional before making any decision regarding treatment of yourself or others.

To request permissions, contact the publisher at publish@joapublishing.com or mrollins@markhamrollins.com

Hardcover ISBN: 978-1-961098-45-9
Paperback ISBN: 978-1-961098-44-2
eBook ISBN: 978-1-961098-46-6
Printed in the USA.

Joan of Arc Publishing
Meridian, ID 83646
www.joapublishing.com

PRAISE FOR MARKHAM F. ROLLINS III

"In the many years I have had the privilege of knowing and loving my husband, I have witnessed firsthand the embodiment of virtues that many aspire to, but few truly achieve. His kindness is not just a trait, but a guiding principle that informs his every action, touching the lives of those around him in the most profound ways. Mark carries a compassion that reaches beyond empathy, extending a hand of understanding and support to all he encounters. He is an inspiration to me and to our whole family. Most importantly, he is a man dedicated to growing as a human being, continually seeking to better himself not just for his own sake, but for the betterment of those around him. His journey of self-improvement and the virtues he upholds are not just topics of this book; they are lived experiences, reflected in his daily life. This book has been a labor of love for Mark. I have watched firsthand as he wrote from his heart with kindness, compassion, and his wonderful caring spirit to bring this book to life and make it something truly extraordinary."

Jody Rollins

Wife, partner, soul mate

"Mark makes it feel accessible to truly be the best version of yourself. He is guided by the simple truth that we are all only on this earth for a short time, and the personal value that we have a responsibility to help each other live our best lives while we can. We all need a Mark Rollins in our lives—that special human being who lives in service to others, always arriving at just the right time and showing up in just the right way as part coach, part everyone's dad, and part friend."

Leslie Gordon

CEO, Food Bank For New York City

"Markham is one of the most caring, energetic, and curious people that I know. His passion to live a life in retirement that is different than his father's led him to continue evolving as both a man and a leader. Whether it's learning about YouTube, AI, or new marketing strategies, I've witnessed his growth mindset firsthand and if there's anyone you want to listen to about how to continue to evolve, it's Markham!"

Evan Carmichael

Speaker, author, YouTube—3.7M subscribers

www.evancarmichael.com

"I met Mark a few years ago in a queue. . .for food!

We live on different sides of the 'pale blue dot' called Earth and sometimes don't speak for many months. Yet when we do, he is a wise and present councillor, mentor, guide, and friend. We pick up where we left off and I always feel a better man by the end of our time together. This book is a reflection of Mark's life, a true dedication to service."

Stew Darling

CEO, Stew Darling Ltd., New Zealand

———————————

"No one is unique. However, Mark is a rare bird. He reads. He ponders. He leans into new experiences and demanding challenges. He asks questions. He pays attention. He stays connected. And so, he is always in the process of becoming a better version of himself. Who better to author a book about the critical need for men to evolve? If you want to keep growing, this is a must-read."

The Rev. Carter V.

———————————

"Unlike some people who prefer to travel solo in their search for meaning and purpose, Mark has always welcomed companionship along the way. I am grateful for the many ways Mark has shown me how vulnerability can lead to strength, conviction, and commitment to make a positive difference. This book is filled with insights and a welcoming invitation for more men to find their best way forward with Mark as an encouraging companion."

Alisa H. Kesten

Social action leader

———————————

"'People will forget what you said, people will forget what you did, but people will never forget how you made them feel.' ~Maya Angelou

We both love this quote. I have known Mark for more than 10 years. Mark is exactly who you see, hear, and come to appreciate. Not sometimes, but all the time. He has a big heart; loves being a servant leader. Family, friends, learning and growing are key aspects of Mark. It's part of his character. Character is a composite of your thoughts, your principles, your actions, your words. An African Proverb says: 'Wherever a man goes to dwell, his character goes with him.' Congratulations and thank you, Mark, for pouring into this book and all that you do. To all the readers, strap in and enjoy your learning journey!"

Dr. Valerie Mason Cunningham

Co-Founder and Co-CEO, Mason & Rice, LLC

"I've had the honor of knowing Mark for many years, and what strikes me most is how he truly lives the principles he shares in The Evolving Man. This isn't just a book for Mark; it's a reflection of his own life's journey. He's more than an author; he's a living example of what it means to evolve continually. His story is one of courage and constant self-reflection. He doesn't just teach about transformation; he's a testament to it. For any man seeking to find a deeper meaning in life, Mark's journey and this book are together a heartfelt invitation to explore and grow. It's not just guidance Mark offers; it's a chance to walk alongside someone who knows what it means to keep evolving."

Bo Eason

Former NFL player, playwright, and speaker

"My fondest memories of Mark revolve around our numerous mission trips to Nicaragua. It started at one of my client's semi-annual networking events when Mark asked if he could share his recent experiences on his most recent mission trip to Nicaragua. He shared his message while a series of pictures were displayed on the screen behind him. At the end, there was not a dry eye in the audience. Returning to the stage, I asked who would be willing to join Mark and me on a mission trip. Well, that turned out to be the first of a dozen trips we completed together. I've been kidding Mark that he turned my life upside down. The first time I mentioned that during a reflection circle at the end of our first trip, his response was, 'Maybe your life has been turned right side up.' There is no doubt that's what happened!"

Roger Sitkins

CEO, Sitkins Group, Inc.

"Mark and I shared a commonality of both being in a family business and being part of the Westchester County, New York business community. We had many conversations about all sorts of topics over the many years of our friendship. His many trips to Nicaragua and his commitment to so many not-for-profits led me to a sincere admiration for his caring personality, belief in a higher power, and strong desire to give back and help those less fortunate. The memory that pops into my head is of his help during a painful divorce. As Mark had a similar experience years prior, his words of encouragement, compassion for both me and my ex-wife, and advice still resonate today."

Joseph Armentano

CEO, Paraco Gas

"Markham is one of those rare individuals who combine real life experience, knowledge and wisdom with real life care, concern and empathy for people. He has a proven track record of success in business and in life. His love for people exudes out of him. His desire to serve and change peoples lives is sincere and genuine. In this book, Markham shares his life-changing insights with his unique enthusiasm and passion that make this book one of most impactful books you will read."

Justin Prince

Entrepreneur, speaker, author

"Mark is the perfect man to write this book. He is obsessed with improvement—both inward and through his communities. Through Mark's anecdotes and narrative, every man will find something insightful and valuable in this book. Finally, the 'why' is the centerpiece of this book: for yourself."

Joan Woodward

President, The Travelers Institute

SPECIAL THANKS AND ACKNOWLEDGEMENTS

This book would not have been possible without the support, love, and kindness my wife, Jody, provided every day as I rose early to write. Her encouragement kept me going for sixteen months, even when I felt I didn't have it in me.

Our children—Markham and his wife, Jennifer; Jonathan and his wife, Mariana, and their two sons, Luca and Camilo; Christopher and his fiancé, Fabio; Evann; Madeline; and Jordan—are all super humans who inspire me every day with who they are. Their support and love for Jody and me amazes me every day.

Thank you to all the 150+ men and others (including women) who provided feedback, answered my emails of journaling questions, and encouraged me to keep going.

And thank you to all the mentors and friends who showed up for me over my lifetime to provide coaching, feedback, and help when I needed it most. Thank you for telling me the things that perhaps I didn't want to hear but needed to hear.

And a personal thank you to my publisher, Keira Brinton, who taught me to channel this book through my heart. You gave me a gift I now use every day. And to my editor, Hanna, who was relentless with suggestions for making my writing easier and better formatted for you, my reader.

TABLE OF CONTENTS

ODE TO A MAN 11

FOREWORD: ABOUT THE BOOK AND WHO IT IS FOR 13

DEDICATION 17

MY JOURNEY SO FAR 19

    INTRODUCTION 21

    BECOMING AN EAGLE SCOUT 23

    WORKING FOR MY DAD 27

    SELLING OUR COMPANY 31

    MY RELATIONSHIP WITH ALCOHOL 35

    MY DIVORCE 39

    THE DAY MY HEART OPENED 43

TWELVE LIFE VIRTUES 47

    INTRODUCTION 49

    LISTENING 51

    VULNERABILITY 61

    HUMILITY 73

    FORGIVENESS 83

    REGRETS 93

    RELATIONSHIPS 103

    GRATITUDE 115

    EGO 125

    COMPASSION AND EMPATHY 135

    CURIOSITY AND LEARNING 145

    KINDNESS AND GENEROSITY 155

    LOVE 165

A DEEPER DIVE 175

    INTRODUCTION 177

    SELF-CARE 179

    SEX AND INTIMACY 189

    MARRIAGE 201

GRIEF 213
SPIRITUALITY 227
LEGACY 239
LETTER FROM MY 90-YEAR-OLD SELF 249

MY FINAL CHALLENGE TO YOU 253
WHAT'S NEXT FOR YOU? 255

ODE TO A MAN

*If ever you are not sure,
then there is work to do.*

*If ever you feel hurt,
then it's time to love yourself.*

*If ever you need help,
look for it.*

*If you think you know all the answers,
then learn more,
better answers will appear.*

*Treat yourself with care, kindness, and love,
do the same to others.*

*Spend time serving others,
your gifts and talents are needed in the world.*

*When other humans cause you harm,
forgiveness can be the healing tool.*

*Living a life with no regrets is possible,
if you own your past digressions
and mistakes as lessons.*

*If you have not written the complete story of your life,
this is the time.*

You are the author, the director, the actor, and the critic in your life.

Leave a legacy that embodies who you truly are.

Markham F. Rollins III

FOREWORD: ABOUT THE BOOK AND WHO IT IS FOR

The Evolving Man is for you if you are looking to grow and evolve to become a better father, son, brother, spouse or partner, friend, and human. This book will not give you any quick fix, but rather will help you start a journey of self-reflection and imagining what a better life could be for you and those around you.

We all get one shot at this life. Why just wander through checking the boxes and calling it in? If you're okay with floating through life, then this book is not for you. But if there is a little voice inside of you asking questions like these, then this book is for you:

- Why do I have such a difficult time listening to people?
- Why do I have a difficult time opening up to share my struggles and look for help?
- Why do I have such a hard time forgiving people?
- How do I let go of all the regrets I carry around?
- Why is the relationship with my spouse becoming flat and boring?
- What would it feel like if I had more gratitude for what I have, instead of desire for what I don't have?
- I'm feeling lonely and I want to find a way to have a community of friends.
- I have a strong ego and am very opinionated, and I think that is hurting my relationships. How do I fix that?
- I have a low capacity for empathy and compassion and I don't know how to fix that.
- What will my legacy be after I am gone?

All of these questions and more are the reasons I wrote *The Evolving Man*. And I commit to you that if you read this and do the work, your life will improve. You will notice the change, and those around you will notice the change as well.

How can I make this commitment to you? Let me give you a little background on *The Evolving Man.* On April 15, 1957, I came into this world and began my journey. I do not know how much longer I will be here, but my vision is to reach 90, then reaccess. My first 66 years have been incredible, and I tell people that I have lived a full life, and if, by chance, my time ends before 90, I'm okay. I am at peace. I am fortunate to have done more than many. I have not lived a perfect life, but I have no regrets. I am quick to forgive, and I do my best to practice unconditional love. I have a wonderful wife and six glorious children, their partners, two grandchildren, and a close circle of family and friends who provide genuine nourishment to my soul. I have suffered just as everyone does. I have made my share of mistakes, and I have learned multiple lessons the hard way. But those lessons have also allowed me to heal and grow into who I am today and to write *The Evolving Man* as a guide for others to do the same.

For example, I was always the person who shied away from controversy, and that trait has not treated me well. It hurt my growth as a leader, a person, a husband, a father, and a friend. It became clear to me that this was a problem early into my second marriage. My wife, Jody, is about as direct as anyone can be. She believes that by not being direct to others, you hinder yourself and others in trying to live a full life. Whenever she was direct with me, I would withdraw, get quiet, and tell her everything was fine, but she knew full-well I did not have the courage to be truthful and tell her how I really felt. I realized I struggled to be vulnerable for fear of shame, judgment, and rejection. Since identifying this, I have worked very hard on not pulling away and retreating. I have come a long way with vulnerability, and still work on it every day. (I have included a whole segment on vulnerability in Section Two where I explain this work further.)

Coming from that place of vulnerability, I wrote *The Evolving Man* entirely from the heart, and it incorporates a number of thoughts that reveal some of my personal philosophies. It is a collection of my own stories, as well as stories of more than 50 other men, just like you and me, who became part of a group I emailed weekly with the same journaling questions you will encounter here. Many of their answers are woven into the fabric of this book, giving you a variety of stories to show you that you are not alone.

This book is for men of all ages. I write it from the perspective of having learned from the mistakes I made along the way as a younger man, and grown from them to where I am now. The purpose of the book is to give you hope, inspiration, guidance, and finally some community that men just seem to get too little of.

In **Section One**, I share with you some major life events that helped shape who I am today. To be clear, my journey still continues and I work on myself every day.

Section Two takes you through 12 life virtues that I feel are critical to spend time on so that you can evolve as a man. Each chapter begins with an overview of the virtue, then a story from my life that was a learning experience for me. As you read this book I will be sharing my stories with you in the hope that you will find the lessons that I have learned too.

As individuals, we all have a personal story that is meaningful and reveals a connection with our own personal growth. Think about it. You wouldn't have remembered your story clearly if it wasn't important. *That means you learned something.* It was a genuine "a-haaa!" moment. And sometimes those stories become suitable tales to share with others because you thought your "lesson" would help them too. I have many stories from throughout my life that have taught me my deepest lessons.

Following that, comes the journaling questions that I asked the 50+ men that were part of the research I did while writing the book. I had more than 2,000 responses to my questions overall. These answers will give you additional perspectives on the topic at hand. Having these different perspectives will let you know that you are not alone with your struggles.

After reading the comments from the men, I give you an opportunity to take these other reflections, stories, and experiences, and then develop your own set of answers to the same questions. This will give you a starting point or an accurate idea of where you stand right now.

Finally, each chapter ends with a challenge for you to grow in that specific area. The challenge may be the most important part and I want to push you to do the work. This book is intended to put you on a path of change.

Section Three covers six more important areas: self-care, sex and intimacy, marriage, grief, spirituality, and then your legacy, using the same format as above. They are not necessarily "virtues," but are important parts of our lives.

In **Section Four**, I spend time with you and explain what to do next; how you can take all that you learned and put it into practice.

Think of this book as a men's discussion group. Pay attention to my opening remarks in each chapter, read what the other men in the room have to say about the topic, then spend time journaling on what your responses would be. Take your time with the journaling. Write it out longhand, using a paper notebook, not a computer. I recommend you jump online, or take a trip to your local bookstore, and get a quality-made, special journal dedicated to this journey. You'll be glad you did.

I am grateful that you purchased this book. If you like it, please buy one for a friend and share what you have learned about yourself with other men. And please feel free to drop me a note; my email is mrollins@markhamrollins.com. I would sincerely love to hear from you.

Download the FREE Workbook

markhamrollins.com

DEDICATION

This book is dedicated to my brother Chuck, to whom I have always looked up to for sound advice and wisdom. He was my younger brother but had the wisdom of an older brother. Chuck was someone for me to admire and learn from.

On August 19th, 2020, Chuck called me to tell me he was just diagnosed with amyotrophic lateral sclerosis, or ALS. We cried together as it sank in, but in typical Chuck fashion he was positive, giving me the sense that he would be okay. His strong spiritual beliefs gave him comfort, which, in turn, gave everyone around him comfort. Thus began his two-year journey with this dreadful disease. His wife Jeanne was always at his side as, day by day, the illness took part of his physical body from him. A daily decline that was brutal and never ending.

None of us know what the end of our lives will be like. In my world, we have lost family members to cancer, dementia, alcoholism, and heart failure. All slow, terrible deaths. Even so, I personally believe that this terrible disease, ALS, is one of the worst ways to exit this life that I can think of.

We all have choices on how we want to live our life. Chuck chose a life of service. Service to our business, service to our families, even service to complete strangers.

I'm dedicating this book to Chuck because he embodied the type of man who has a strong moral ethic and foundation in all the virtues I write about in this book. We all can up our game to become more like Chuck; to become the type of man that creates a following so strong that he will be talked about for decades. He touched the lives of thousands of people with his mentoring, coaching, sound advice, and—above all—his incredible gift of being the best listener that I have known.

18

SECTION 1
MY JOURNEY SO FAR

SECTION 1

INTRODUCTION

This section is a little about me and my journey so far. I want you to better understand me so that you can see where I am coming from when I write about each life virtue. We are all individual men with our own skills, emotions, and good and bad habits that make us who we are.

And we all have the capacity to change. I certainly have changed a lot over my first 66 years here, and expect to keep changing and evolving.

As you read the next six chapters and learn more about me, I challenge you to think and write about yourself in this same way:

- ☐ What are some pivotal moments in your life that helped influence who you are today?
- ☐ Who are some of the people that impacted your life?
- ☐ What are some areas of your life that you know that need change?

Think back on your childhood, your education, your time in college if you went, and your career. Think of loved ones who have passed away and your most important relationships.

If you are not used to journaling or writing, this might be challenging. I want to encourage you to get comfortable writing in your journal about your past, about your feelings, and about your dreams. Over the course of time, I have found that men are hesitant to show their true emotions. This is not news to most people because for centuries, men have been expected to be strong, to be tough, to not "let their guard down," and if they need to cry about something, they will usually do it privately. But why does this expectation exist?

Personally, I believe men should do the complete opposite, and be at peace in their emotions. There are plenty of emotional men who are just as solid in character as the "tough guys." I cry during OnStar commercials and sad movies, and I'm okay with that.

It takes a strong man to be able to show vulnerability and emotions in a way that society would want to be critical of, and that's a shame. Women don't have a monopoly on expression, and men need to be comfortable in their own skin too. As I contemplated this idea more, it soon became one of the first premises for this book.

Before we move onto the next chapter, spend a few minutes to start thinking and writing about your journey up until now. Think of it as a history of your life or a highlight reel. Make it fun and, as you write, sink into your feeling of joy and happiness for all that you have accomplished so far and who you are as a man, a father, a brother, a son, or a husband.

CHAPTER 2

BECOMING AN EAGLE SCOUT

The Scout Oath:

On my honor I will do my best to do my duty to God and my country and to obey the Scout Law; to help other people at all times; to keep myself physically strong, mentally awake, and morally straight.

The Scout Law:

A Scout is trustworthy, loyal, helpful, friendly, courteous, kind, obedient, cheerful, thrifty, brave, clean, and reverent.[1]

---

[1] Boy Scouts of America n/d. "What are the Scout Oath and Scout Law?" Scouting.org. Accessed 2023. https://www.scouting.org/about/faq/question10/.

On one of our weekend camping trips, I remember sitting with my Scoutmaster as his tanned leathery hands worked a needle and waxed thread through the birch bark that he asked me to strip from a tree in the woods with my knife. As he carefully folded the bark and held it in one hand, the other hand did his magic. I watched him create for me a miniature birch canoe about nine inches long. As he was pulling the thread through the holes he had made with his awl, he looked up and, with his deep voice, mentored me.

- How are you enjoying camping this summer?
- What has been the best part?
- How many merit badges do you have?
- You are about halfway to getting Eagle Scout; do you think you can do it?
- Is there anything I can do to help you get there?

This was my first interaction with an older man (besides my dad) who was curious, kind, compassionate, and willing to nurture me along a path of growth.

During the vulnerable ages of 10 to 18, I was an active member of Troop 2 in Mamaroneck, New York. Mr. Armand Lancia was our Scoutmaster and we had about 50 kids in the troop, so there was plenty of opportunity for leadership roles. Mr. Lancia had a huge impact on my life, as did his son, Steve Lancia, who is still a friend to this day.

It was during those years that I first learned crucial life skills that I still use today. The memories are vivid as I think back on all of the hiking, camping (summer and winter), canoe trips and portages, horseback riding, riflery, open fire cooking, and leadership growth. Scouting gave me the discipline I needed at that time in my life. For example, we all had to practice the discipline of getting up early to the sound of a trumpet playing Reveille, and Taps played at sunset gave me the habit of going early to bed.

The merit badges I earned gave me exposure to other life skills and interests. Camping, canoeing, woodworking, first aid, cooking, personal fitness, lifesaving, and citizenship are just some of the 21 merit badges that are required to achieve the rank of Eagle. I also studied and earned the God and Country designation. All these merit badges—all of the work to move from Tenderfoot up the highest rank of Eagle—gave me a strong base from which to grow as a young man.

Scouting led me into more outdoor adventures that all helped to sculpt me into who I am. I learned to hunt large and small game, I was an avid fisherman, camper, and downhill skier. All those experiences are part of who I am today. I no longer do any of these activities, but have important memories of very specific moments in my life.

Hunting taught me I do not like to kill. Camping taught me I could survive in the woods if I had to, but I prefer a nice hotel or my own home. Fishing taught me I have patience, but again I had trouble with the killing.

As my three boys came of age, we tried scouting again for them. I became the assistant Scoutmaster and founded a new troop in Bedford, New York with Dr. Gary Cohn, an avid Scouter with sons similar in age to mine. The troop was small, and my boys did not have the same passion as I did, so over time we fell away. But, all my own years in Scouting helped me with such important foundational life skills. I am forever grateful for Armond Lancia, his son Steve, and the other 50 young men who were with me during these formative years. To this day, I live by the Scout Oath and Scout Law. It was building block number one for me.

CHAPTER 3

WORKING FOR MY DAD

My mom gave me a kiss as I walked out the door to drive to my first day of work. I was wearing the Brooks Brothers suit and tie she bought for me that summer. I also had in my hand the tan leather, monogrammed briefcase from the same store. It was rectangular, had a sturdy handle, was about 4" deep with pockets inside for my pens, business cards, and pads, and a spot for my calculator. It had shiny brass clips that I would slide away from the center to open it. *Click, click. Click, click.* I can still hear that sound. I used that briefcase for 15 years.

As I drove the 25 minutes from Mamaroneck where I grew up, to Bronxville, New York, where our family insurance agency was, I had a feeling of excitement and a strong feeling of responsibility since I was going to be the fourth generation of Rollins's to work there. It was started in 1910 by my great grandfather, Marland W. Rollins.

On this first day of work, I was following my dad, who was in his car, as he led me to the local Gulf gas station parking lot down the street from the office. My dad was 47 years old, and I was 23. As we walked the short distance to the office, the streets were empty as it was still only 6:30 a.m.. The office opened for business at 9:00, but we had to be the first ones in. That was my first lesson. "You have to be the first one in, make the coffee, go get the mail at the post office, and get the office ready for everyone else."

My dad was a U.S. Marine and while he, thankfully, never served overseas, he was a Marine in his heart and soul. I was born at Camp Lejeune in North Carolina, and I think I inherited some of his character by way of blood relation. His mantra was, *"Work hard, play hard, and always help those less fortunate."* The "work hard" portion of that always took precedence over everything else.

My dad showed me to my office where there was a huge, black metal desk with a Formica imitation-wood desktop. There was a new yellow pages phone book and three Hagstrom Map atlases for the three counties surrounding our office. It was our form of GPS in that day. There was a phone with six buttons along the bottom for outgoing calls, an electric plug-in calculator with a tape, and a few pads and pens. I put my Brooks Brothers briefcase on the desk, and we headed to the kitchen to make coffee.

At that time, my dad had three very good friends who were also his business partners. Nat, Ed, and Kurt started to stroll in around 7:00 to 7:30 a.m. They always grabbed a cup of coffee and headed to my dad's office where the four of them had coffee time until 8:30. It was there, during these meetings, that they joked, laughed, and made decisions on the business. I was included in the meeting that day, and most of the talk focused on what they were going to do with me.

There was no training program. There was also no clear path forward. There was no learning program, no computers, no cell phones. But there were six secretaries who sat in a row of desks down the middle of the room. All the desks had IBM Selectric typewriters, as well as phones, calculators, and, of course, *ashtrays*, which were still a sign of the times. One by one, the secretaries came into my office that day to meet the "heir-apparent." Ed gave me the nickname "the kid" and it stuck, so that's what they called me.

On my way back from the post office carrying a huge load of mail, I was amazed at the volume of the clicking sound of the typewriters and the plumes of smoke coming from the secretaires who all had 1980s hairstyles sitting high on their heads. It was just like a scene out of the popular drama TV series *Mad Men* with Don Draper.

According to my dad, the mail was critical to our survival as a business. As I opened it, I had to sort it by putting all the checks in one pile, insurance policies for clients in another, claims in a third, and a final pile for general correspondence. My dad scanned each pile and then I had to distribute them to our bookkeeper, claims manager, and office manager. Thus began my 38-year career in our family business.

For the next 38 years, I went from opening the mail to becoming the CEO. On that journey, we grew from about $1,000,000 in revenue to over $6,000,000. But it was really when my dad retired in 1998 at the age of 65 that the biggest change took place. My brother Chuck and I bought him out and totally transformed what was a nice, small-town, family-owned insurance agency into a regional firm that was admired by many of our competitors and clients.

Working for my dad had its challenges. Anyone reading this who has been in a multi-generational family business understands the benefits and the struggles of this kind of work environment. It is wonderful in so many ways, and also brings with it family dynamics that, at times, can feel stressful as you and other family members navigate your roles in the company.

All the learning that I did over those 38 years has positioned me well for this phase of my life, and I'm grateful to every teammate who I worked with.

CHAPTER 4

SELLING OUR COMPANY

The email arrived in my inbox around 4:30 p.m. on Friday June 7th, 2013. It read, "Gentlemen, the deal has closed, the final documents are attached, and the money has been wired to your account. Congratulations! On behalf of the entire leadership team of Brown and Brown, Inc. (BRO), we are excited to have you as part of our team. Have a wonderful weekend."

Chuck and I both received that same email upon selling the company that was founded by our great grandfather, Marland W. Rollins. He started the insurance brokerage in 1910 in Bronxville, New York. As fourth generation owners, it was on us to decide its future. Our combined six children had no interest in taking it over, and we knew we would sell to an outsider. I was 56 at the time, Chuck was 54, and although I fully intended to work until I was 65, it felt that the time was right to cash out and invest the proceeds. From there, we could give the new company 10 more years of our lives then retire and enjoy our retirement.

As I read that email, there was a sense of relief. Finally, this process was behind us and I could get on with my life. There was also the feeling of, *"Did I do the right thing?"* For me, my family, our clients, and our strategic partners it all felt fine. But for my ancestors . . . what would Marland say if he were here?

The very next day, I bought myself a Rolex Submariner watch as a gift to myself for all the work Chuck, our team, and I did to build the company since buying it from our dad in 1998. I wear that watch every day. To this day, when I look at it, I think of the 103 years our company provided services to generations of families and businesses, as well as to the teammates who worked with us for their entire careers. There were also a number of nonprofit organizations that we supported over the years, and I was satisfied that we had done our best for everyone involved.

The weekend was filled with quiet celebrations. Some of it was spent dreaming about what would be coming next for us, and some was spent thinking about the reality that we had just ended a fourth-generation family business. Our company was a true rarity, as only a very small percentage of all family businesses make it that far.

On the following Monday morning at 9:00, Chuck and I called a meeting for our entire team of 25. Only three people knew what we had done, as we had needed their help along the way. To put it mildly, selling to a public company is complicated. It must be done with a veil of secrecy, and it always takes longer than anyone expects or wants. We had a team of lawyers, a mergers and acquisitions firm, our accounting firm, and each other to navigate through all the poking and prodding of our financials, our history, our pro forma analysis, and much more.

For weeks, Chuck and I had practiced what we would say to our work family. We were fully prepared to be positive, energetic, succinct, and clear with our words, so we could deliver a beautiful picture of the future. While we delivered our well rehearsed speeches, we were not prepared for the loud gasps, the hands that quickly covered mouths, or the crying that filled the room as our comments flowed into the room of shocked listeners.

Comments like *"I can't believe you are doing this," "Why are you doing this?", "What will happen to me?", "Who will I report to now?"* filled the room. We did the best we could to answer everyone's questions and calm any fears. I even had to calm my own fears that were building in me as we were peppered with questions from teammates who were more like family. Even though we guaranteed that no one would lose their job, they felt abandoned, betrayed, and, frankly, out of a job.

After what felt like an eternity, we ended the meeting. And as we repeatedly said, we would be available to talk to anyone who needed to talk more. For the rest of the day there was a never-ending line out my door as I counseled everyone who needed to talk and learn more. But it was the ones who I thought for sure would come in, but didn't, that I was most worried about.

As Chuck and I called our largest clients to give them the news before they read about it online, something magical happened. Instead of fear, anxiety, and concern, we heard

- *"That's exciting, is this good for you?"*
- *"Are you going to stay on?"*
- *"Is my account manager staying?"*

They were happy for us and showed none of the concern that we had anticipated. It was a ray of sunshine on a day that was causing me to need a drink in the worst possible way.

For the next five years we grew our company threefold from $6,000,000 in revenue to $18,000,000, and from 25 employees to 80. There was turnover for sure, but in the end it all settled down and the company continues to this day under the leadership of my friend John, who I had mentored for years.

Once I sold our company, there was a huge identity shift that was difficult at times. It was something I was not prepared for, and I had trouble processing the change. I had spent 38 years building my brand and my identity. And overnight, seemingly most of that was gone. Sure, I was still a leader, a great salesperson, a good father, and a good husband. Much of who I was moved through the transaction with me, mostly intact, but some did not. I was no longer the CEO of my own company. I was now a regional leader for one of the 150 Brown and Brown offices in the USA.

My original plan was to work until I was 65 or maybe even longer. But after three years at the helm, which included integrating 60 people from the four acquisitions, I was more than a little burned out. So, I stepped down to slide into an easier role of serving my 25 largest clients. It was a role I had been in before we sold, but instead of feeling a sense of relief I instantly became bored. It was as if I had become irrelevant, and I felt lost.

For the next 12 months I did the best I could to find and accept my new role at the company. But my identity had changed, my responsibilities were minimal, and I no longer had a say in the day to day operations. It was a difficult time for me and I found myself disengaged from the business. I was going in late and coming home early which all led to unhealthy habits and a sense of emptiness with no real purpose in life. I was scared and knew that I had to make a change.

It was those feelings that led me to retire in December of 2018. In fact, it was the same day that my wife Jody retired from her senior-level position at Chubb. Our journey together since then has been marvelous and I imagine will be written about in my next book.

CHAPTER 5

MY RELATIONSHIP WITH ALCOHOL

My 1968 maroon Plymouth Barracuda was filled to the brim with everything I thought I needed for my freshman year at The University of Hartford in Connecticut. I picked this college for two reasons. For one, it was only 80 miles from my home in New York, so I could head back home whenever I felt the need. The second reason was that I was destined to join the family insurance business as a fourth-generation family owner, and the University of Hartford offered an insurance-major in their business school.

Back then it was a small university with about 4,000 undergrads. They were better known for their music school, and their arts school, but the business school had what I needed.

As I pulled up in front of my dorm, dozens of senior classmen were there to help bring all my stuff up to the fourth floor. There was no elevator, so it took a long time and I remember it was hot and steamy that day. Once everything was in place, I came back down to rent a refrigerator. I needed to have a place to keep my Budweiser. Once that was in our room, I ran out to get a cold case so I could let the celebration begin with my new roommates.

All I had were their names and home addresses. Back then, there was no such thing as social media to learn more about who they were, what they looked like, or who else was in their group of friends. I didn't know them, but I just assumed that they were as thirsty as I was for a cold one. When I walked into the room with the cold case of beer on my shoulder, there was Charlie and his mom Betty. Charlie had a look of excitement on his face; his mom not so much.

Once all the parents had cleared the rooms, the drinking began. Saturday morning was my first college hangover and I became intimately familiar with our toilet as I threw up several times. Back then we called it the "Porcelain God," as we prayed to him to make us feel better. But a quick walk to the cafeteria for some greasy bacon and eggs set me straight.

My dad was a big drinker and encouraged my brother Chuck and my sister Susan to drink at a young age. For Chuck and me, it was long days of chores around the house, always followed up by some cold beers because that's what hard working men did. So, by 15 I was already sneaking into bars. The drinking age was 18 back then instead of 21, and the bars were more flexible than they are today.

During high school, we had no problem drinking and driving. If you got pulled over, the police would ask you to drive home as they followed. It was their job to ring the doorbell, wake my parents, and share the news that I was out drinking underage and driving as well. It was my parents' responsibility to teach me a lesson and straighten me out. It was not handled through the application of laws at the time.

That early teaching by my dad set me on a path of self-destruction that luckily never ended in tragedy. I came close in my junior year of college, driving home from a late night in the school pub when I fell asleep and ran into a snowbank. I woke up as the car launched into the air and landed with a huge thump in the parking lot of a gas station. I was very clearly shaken, and I limped home at 10 miles an hour with two flat tires and steam coming out from under the hood.

This was not the first time this happened. Early in my freshman year, I was missing my girlfriend Joan back in Mamaroneck. So, at 9:00 on a Friday night I grabbed a six pack and drove the 80 miles home to surprise her. Twice I was rattled awake by my car running onto the shoulder. I finally made it home at about 11:00, with a pretty good buzz on, only to find out she had a new boyfriend and our relationship was over.

Fast forward to today and as I think back, I am one of the lucky ones. Early in my first marriage and career I was a party animal. Still intimately involved with the early-morning puking and day-long hangovers. As my children started middle school, I made a pact with myself to stop drinking for a while. I went day by day just saying I am not going to drink today. This went on for three years and it was the best I felt in a very long time. My dad at that point was an alcoholic and his behavior began to change, and I was worried about me, and my children. I was protecting my children and myself by being a better role model.

When I think back on those three years of sobriety, they were the best I have ever felt. My head was clear, and I began to understand alcoholism more and tried talking with my dad about his drinking. We came very close to having an intervention, but I could not get enough close friends and family to support doing one. My dad worsened and my brother and I made the decision to keep our children from him. It was difficult, and while we still saw my mom, we were afraid of the effect his behavior might have on our children. Slowly over time we reentered his world, but with strict boundaries.

When Jody and I first got married in 2009, she had three beautiful daughters. Evann was 10 years old, and the twins, Madeline and Jordan, were both 8. Our jobs were demanding, and we took turns grocery shopping on the way home at night. We loved cooking together and that took place at around 6:00 with a bottle of white wine. When dinner was ready and that bottle was empty, we opened a bottle of red. We always chose one of our favorites and had that with dinner. On occasion, after the kids had left the table to do their homework, we would open another bottle to have "one more glass."

That was normal for us, and we did not think much about it. But I do remember those days well, and that I always woke up with a headache. My mind was often foggy in the morning and I usually needed at least three cups of black coffee to clear my head and start my day.

As I aged, I developed some health scares, one of which was high blood sugar. My naturopath doctor walked me through the sugar levels in foods and alcohol and thus ended my love for wine. After about three years of no alcohol (my third time), I decided that maybe I was missing out and, to the surprise of many, I ordered a wine while out at dinner one night at one of our favorite restaurants. We had the kids with us and while everyone was supportive of me not drinking, they also jumped with joy as I took my first sip in a long time of the Far Niente Cabernet sitting on the table. One of my favorites. The funny thing was as I took a sip, it burned as it went down. Not anything I remember at all! I forced myself to finish it. The next morning, that hangover feeling was there—the headache, the lack of clarity, a little guilt—and it brought me back to every hangover I have had since my first one at 15.

My early experience with alcohol has helped me to understand why some people drink. If I was sad or depressed, I would drink to numb that pain. If I was happy and up for a good time, I would drink to celebrate with my friends. As I got older, I moved from beer to vodka to wine. I fell in love with Chardonnay, Pinot Noir, Cabernet, and more. I researched different blends and always enjoyed wine with my meals. But my problem was that I could never get enough.

Today, I will still have a glass of wine, but usually only on special occasions. This may mean once a month or so. But no matter what, I always get that burning sensation. I'm truly thankful that I am better at recognizing how my body feels, and I am able to make better decisions as a result.

As we age, I believe our bodies respond more adversely to excessive alcohol. There are studies that say one glass of wine a night can be helpful, and it's precisely those studies that give people the excuse they need to drink to their own satisfaction. And I am okay with that. It's a personal choice, and all I suggest is that you think about your own relationship with alcohol and pay attention to how your body feels when you drink, especially the day after. Do what works best for you and, if you think you have a problem, take it seriously and get some help.

CHAPTER 6

MY DIVORCE

We were sitting down at the kitchen dining table about to have dinner. I was watching her move around the kitchen preparing our dinner and putting the final touches on what was going to be a great meal. She was a great cook and did it with care and love. We were alone that night as we had recently become empty nesters for the first time. Our three sons were all away at school.

As she sat down, Sally, my wife at the time, looked at me and asked what was wrong. I was staring at her, trying to look deep into her soul to find a connection, and I was having trouble. I could not figure out why I felt the way I did and was unsettled.

As I looked across the table, I felt that the only strong tie we really had was our children, and they were gone. We had grown apart, at least in my view. My life, my beliefs, my interests had all changed from when we first got married 25 years earlier.

Our therapist, Jay, gave us a great analogy that I still share every time I talk to people about my divorce. He said that married couples are like two railroad tracks. And while they may be going side by side in the same direction, people do change, and the tracks tend to widen over time as people change. I think I had changed more than my wife and it was me that was feeling out of place in this relationship.

Jay went on to say that what holds a relationship together are the railroad ties. These are the things that people have in common. These include things like interests, hobbies, passions, etcetera. For us, the biggest railroad tie—the one that is everlasting, the one that is unbreakable—was our children. But at that point, we were empty nesters, and that tie became unsettled as our children were finding their way through college and their careers. They were gone from the home, and it was just us. That's when therapy started and we began the difficult and heart-breaking task of unwinding our relationship.

After 25 years of marriage, and then many months of counseling, I knew it was not going to work going forward. But how would I tell our kids? How would I tell our family and friends? How could this be happening to us? Was there a way for me to live the life that we built together even though I felt we had moved so far apart?

It was the hardest decision I had ever made in my life. And I know I caused pain for my entire family, for which I am sorry. I suppose you could say I was being selfish in a way . . . I was more about my own life and being happy than I was about everyone else. I knew I needed a change, and that I was looking for something more. The process was difficult for everyone. My mother- and father-in-law, Jayne and Alan, were my best friends. When we told them, they understood and said no matter what they would always welcome me into their house. I believed them, but still over the next 10 years there was a noticeable strain on all the relationships.

Ultimately, we did get separated and divorced. The boys are fine. Sally and I had always put the boys first, and they had grown into amazing young men. We attend family events together and always find time to chat about any big issues with the boys.

When we got married, I was 25 and she was 21. I have always wondered if that was too young. We did the best we could and raised three great young men, made many friends along the way and were living a good life together. But deep in my heart and soul, I was out of alignment. The time of the divorce was difficult for sure, and I lost some friends. My kids were confused at times, and of course they were sad. We were *all* sad, and I used the event as a learning experience. I don't regret that our marriage did not last, but I did learn a lot about relationships. I will admit that I was the one who pulled away, and it was because I had changed so much and was looking for a different life.

I am remarried now to my soulmate. Jody is my business partner, my life partner, and more. She came to the marriage with more than I expected. She is loving, kind, smart, funny, and she cares deeply about my sons. They have two mothers, with different perspectives and parenting styles. Jody also brought her amazing three daughters, Evann, Jordan, and Madeline, who I treat as my own daughters, and my sons treat them like sisters.

Before we got married, we did see a marriage counselor at my suggestion. I wanted to learn from my mistakes and make sure this marriage lasted. We learned some great tools and strategies for communication, kindness, empathy, and more. Jody and I are always trying to learn new ways to deepen and widen our love for each other, our children, our family at large, and our friends.

We talk to our children about the risks of marriage. Right now, the divorce rate in the USA is down so that's a good trend. We encourage our children to really go deep in their relationships and build as many ties as they can with their partner. We also encourage them to meet with a counselor to learn communication techniques that will strengthen their relationships.

When you read the chapter on marriage you will hear from other men who have failed marriages. As well from men whose marriages have lasted through the tests of time. My second marriage is not without challenges, but our open communication has allowed us to continue to grow as a couple, and stay grounded and in love. As you read more of this book, many of the chapters will help you find ways to be a better husband—the kind every partner wants.

CHAPTER 7

THE DAY MY HEART OPENED

I had been crouching for about an hour, moving down the wall, cleaning up the concrete between the rows of cinder blocks that were placed there by one of the high school students. As I looked across the worksite, I noticed Maria, one of the local women who we recently built a home for on my last trip. My Spanish was limited but we always found a way to communicate. She was about 22 years old and had three children ages 6 months, 2 years, and 4 years old. Her husband worked as a day laborer cutting sugarcane and was paid about $3 USD a day. In Nicaragua men and women marry as young as 14 and begin families right away.

Maria was standing at the edge of the road about 30 feet from where we were all working. There were several other villagers watching, but Maria was looking more interested in what we were all doing. Jim Gordon—one of the founders of Bridges to Community, which was an NGO from New York—ran trips to Nicaragua. It was primarily a community-development and house-building organization, and we were building a church in the village of Las Conchitas. Jim and his wife Bonnie served as our hosts and liaisons with everyone in the village. Jim noticed Maria and headed over to talk to her. She held a special place in Jim's and Bonnie's hearts. After a brief discussion, some smiles, and a hug, Maria got to work. She really wanted to help, and Jim said it would be okay.

Maria kept walking back and forth, one cinder block in each hand, carrying them from the street to the middle of the worksite. She had no gloves and wore flip flops on her feet as she trudged over the dry earth and around the pourings of wet cement. It was late morning, so the sun was not quite yet at its peak level in the sky. And although we did have some shade, it was already a hot day. We all had clothing that, by now, was sticking to our skin. There was a strong breeze that day, and the dry earth made for recurring dust bowls sending dirt into every crevice on our bodies.

At the time, I was 42 years old with three sons, two of whom were there on this trip. This was my second visit in two years, and I had committed the previous year to come back every year and bring more people with me to live this experience.

But *this* trip was special. We had a fresh crew of students, and it allowed me to relive my first trip through their eyes. Ten of the students were from the Bedford Presbyterian Church in Bedford Village, New York, and the other 10 were from Temple Shaaray Tefila located in the same village. There were several adult leaders as well.

It was at that moment, as Maria was bringing back two more blocks, that I began to well up inside. It was a feeling I had never had before, and I was not sure what was happening. As I continued to watch Maria, I looked to my left and saw that Jim Gordon was there at my side.

With tears in my eyes, I shared with Jim what was going on and how I was feeling. I described in detail the feeling of sadness, happiness, humility, gratitude, and joy, all at the same time. The feeling of love and respect for Maria and the rest of her family, and for the people in this small village, was overwhelming. He stared back at me and said, "What you are feeling is the way God intended for all humans to feel. And imagine what the world would be like, if all humans felt the way you are feeling right now."

It was then that I began my journey towards living a life filled with unconditional love. As I think back, not only on that specific trip, but the next 20 trips to Nicaragua and the Dominican Republic to build homes for families living on the edge of survival, I realize now that there is a different way to weave ourselves through life. A way led by love and the belief in a higher power. I talk more about this in the chapter on spirituality.

SECTION 2
TWELVE LIFE VIRTUES

SECTION 2

INTRODUCTION

We all tend to know what our values are, and to live our lives according to how they align with who we are and who we want to be. We learn the basics at a young age which include principles like knowing right from wrong, being kind to others, treating others as you would like to be treated, etcetera. Many of these were taught to us by our parents, our families, our school systems, our religious establishments, or our spiritual leaders. I learned from all those sources, and am grateful for all the people who provided mentorship along the way.

As I moved through my career, and was raising a family, it became my turn to mentor others on their personal journeys. As the expression goes, "the best way to learn something is to teach it." This section is part learning for myself, part teaching you so that you can learn. It takes shared experience and shared learning to truly make progress when we need to make a change in our lives.

Towards the beginning of this book, I briefly mentioned the Boy Scout

Law, which is comprised of 12 virtues that a Scout must strive to live up to (trustworthy, loyal, helpful, friendly, courteous, kind, obedient, cheerful, thrifty, brave, clean, and reverent). It's a way of living that was taught to me over and over for eight years. Those principles are truly ingrained into my everyday life. But that was not enough for me, nor would it be for you. In this section, we are going to look at some of what is in the Scout Law, but also some other core values that, if practiced on a regular basis, will uplift your life. They will put you on a path of self-alignment, they will bring you peace of mind, they will help you heal if that is needed, and they will become part of your very fabric as a human being.

Let's talk about change. Some people are set in their ways and will continue through the rest of their lives as they are today. Some may have purchased this book and never even got to this section. And that's fine, we can't help everyone, especially those that don't want or think they need change. But if you are reading this now, then you are one of the men who can see a brighter future. A man who can see that, with a little effort and small incremental changes in beliefs and behaviors, you can improve your life and the lives of those around you. Congratulations on being one of those men!

Having the right mindset will make the difference in whether you improve your life, or you don't. Go at your pace and set aside time to do the work at the end of each chapter. Even if you think you may have that core value dialed in, go deeper. We have one shot at this life. We can be as grateful as we can for what we have today, but there is always more. Dream big, and live hard.

Download the FREE Workbook

markhamrollins.com

CHAPTER 8

LISTENING

Take a moment and think back to the last time you were speaking with someone and they were really listening. They were looking you in the eye, perhaps nodding their head once in a while, hanging onto each and every word that came out of your mouth. They made you so at ease that you told them more than you even wanted to. There was a warmth about them that made you feel heard and cared for. They did not interrupt you, they did not rush to judgment or attempt to fix your problem. They allowed for silence between your thoughts. And at the end of your conversation, there may have been some thoughtful encouragement or questions to draw out more. For me, it was always like that with my brother Chuck. When I was speaking with him, even if we were in a crowded room, as far as he was concerned, I was the only person there.

And as far as I'm concerned, listening is the most important virtue in this book. And, at the same time, the hardest to learn. If there is one thing you get from reading this book, it must be the art of listening. Even a 10% improvement will have a profound effect on your life and the lives around you. It is by far the greatest gift you can give to someone else. It is an act of love, kindness, gratitude, appreciation, humility, and so much more.

If you can master this virtue, the rest of the virtues come easier. Your ability to let those you care about most feel heard, seen, and understood, will bring you closer to them and improve your relationships in all areas of your life. I will tell you up front this will be hard. Listening must be practiced and honed for life with relentless effort. The journey to becoming a good listener will be difficult, but the payback will be huge.

My story

My client was explaining about the new product they were bringing to market. It was a medical device that would help their customers provide a new level of life safety to their client population. They were talking about the steps they were taking to make sure all risk management practices that we had recommended were put in place. There were five other people at the table along with Erica—my colleague and the senior account manager—who was writing notes as fast as people were speaking.

It was July of 2017, and probably my thirtieth annual four-day trip visiting my largest client, located in Stavanger, Norway. This was our stewardship meeting to get any updates on their company and any new risks that we should be concerned about. But something was different this year. For the first time, I felt distant and detached from the meeting. It probably stemmed from the fact I had sold my company five years earlier and, having stepped down as office leader, I was beginning to wonder about my future and how much longer I could work.

My mind was wandering to thoughts of retirement. No more meetings, no more busy schedules, no more annual trips to Norway. Then, Ingvald, the treasurer, asked me for the second time, "What do you think Mark?" We were friends and he trusted my advice and counsel, and I was letting him down by not paying attention. I quickly regrouped and jumped back into the conversation.

That night in my hotel room I realized that I needed to leave my current job. There was no way I could continue with this lackadaisical attitude and inability to focus any more on deep work conversations. A mistake could be made, causing financial harm to my clients and teammates.

When I arrived back from Norway, I met with my boss, Tony, and let him know I needed to end my career with Brown and Brown. We agreed I would retire in May of 2018. That would give us a year to find my replacement and have me unwind from my role as president of that office. But by the end of 2017, I agreed to extend until December 2018.

The point of this story is, this example of poor listening is only one aspect of the danger of not paying attention to those around you.

Another example of what poor listening can look like is me not really paying attention to what someone is saying but instead thinking of what my response will be, even before they have finished speaking. When I anticipate what I am going to say and can't wait to share my thoughts, I inevitably shut down the conversation. This is one of my worst habits. It can be destructive to your closest relationships.

When I committed to marrying Jody, I swore to myself that I would really listen better. I would say before that, I was a 5 out of 10 on the listening proficiency scale. Today, I would rate myself a 7 out of 10. Do I think I will ever be a perfect 10? Anyone who knows anything about perfecting a craft, knows that as you improve, "perfection" gets further and further away. It's what is known as an "ever-receding horizon," and it plays an important role in one's development of any skill. So, the scale will change as I improve, and my perfection horizon will recede. Listening is a lifelong skill that needs constant monitoring and improvement. But it is worth the work. When I am really listening to Jody, my kids, or my friends, devoting my full attention and waiting to formulate answers makes a dramatic difference in the quality of our entire conversation. Many times, these close relationships are not looking for advice or suggestions, they just want to be heard. They want a genuine reply that indicates I am invested in what they have to say. They want the respect of knowing that their communication is valued.

This is especially true of me and Jody. When we truly listen to each other—with no judgment, no interruption or reply that comes too early, and no reactive suggestions—our love truly deepens. We become closer, and we grow and learn more about each other. We take care to consider that we are both lifelong learners, and the new knowledge we acquire helps to shape our beliefs and feelings. It's important to listen to what each other is thinking, and not shut each other down.

Listening is a skill that can be learned and nurtured over time. Once you start really listening, listening to others is probably the greatest gift you can give to someone. I try hard every day to improve my listening skills. I know I am being a good listener when the other person is more open to talking and sharing.

What do others have to say?

Here are some important questions with actual responses from other men like you:

Does listening come easy for you? Why or why not?

"It is not something that comes easily to me. I work at it, but it is something that I need to do better. I find myself sometimes cutting people off in the middle of their sentences if I disagree with them or if I am passionate about the topic being discussed."

James W.

"Depends who is speaking. Sometimes yes, and sometimes I tune out. Especially if I have previous experience with the speaker. I am told that I also interrupt. I find my mind ahead of the speaker—like I know what they are going to say— so I either tune out or interrupt."

Ted K.

"Listening does not come easy for me. I might look at the person that is talking to me and know they are talking, but I don't hear them. Basically that is because usually my mind is on something else."

Charles W.

How have your listening skills helped or hurt your relationships?

"With my wife, I think I often fail at active listening and that, of course, hurts the relationship. I have some preconceived notions of what is being said, which can be way off base. If I just slow down and be more thoughtful, things are better. I want to jump into action and fix things so if she isn't feeling great, I want to fix it. But really all she's looking for is someone to listen and acknowledge feelings."

Anonymous

"I am a problem-solver and immediately jump to solutions, and many times skip the empathy/sympathy response that the person is likely looking for. This irritates my wife since many times my wife just wants to be heard."

Anonymous

"One memory regarding the difference good and bad listening can make comes to mind. Several years ago while visiting our married daughter, her middle son (then aged 6 or so) came over to the chair where I was reading and he asked some questions which I now forget. Without missing a beat, I laid down my book and zoomed in on him. 'Sure, Jack, what do you want?' From the kitchen I heard my 38-year-old daughter say, 'You never listened to me that intently when I was his age!' So true, so sad."

Kevin C.

What are some of the ways in which you practice good listening?

"Eye contact is essential. Also, setting aside devices such as the phone, iPad, or laptop is important to engage in good listening. Head nodding and confirmation of what is being said helps the other person know you are 'all in' on the conversation. Lastly, once a person is finished making their point it can be reassuring to them if you summarize a few key points they just made. This helps them know they have been heard. I use this approach particularly when a person is making a complaint or venting."

David C.

"I practice good listening by focusing on what's being said, not anticipating what someone is going to say, since not everyone thinks the way we ourselves do. I go deeper and ask a follow-up question to get them to amplify what they said. It shows I am paying attention and that I genuinely want to understand what they are saying."

Anonymous

"I have recently been trying to be more communicative about how I am feeling going into a conversation. Sometimes your partner wants to have a deeper conversation or wants your advice on a very serious thing, and that can be challenging when you are not in the right mental space to be the sounding board that they need you to be."

Keith B.

Any other thoughts on listening?

"Listening is the highest form of loving. So I try to have my whole body be available to receive what they're sharing and make them feel heard."

Seth S.

"Listening is perhaps one of the most underappreciated relationship skills. I have sat through countless meetings and holiday dinners where people just talk over one another again and again. Becoming a more attentive, focused listener will improve the quality and depth of your relationships."

Anonymous

"When you are tasked with listening to a loved one and trying to offer support, you are taking on an important responsibility. You are helping them work through something. They are relying on you. If you are not up to the task, it is important to say as much, despite how difficult it may be to say so."

Keith B.

Your Turn:

If you want the best results possible from this book, answer the journaling questions before moving onto the next section.

Does listening come easy for you? Why or why not?

_____
_____
_____
_____
_____

How have your listening skills helped or hurt your relationships?

_____
_____
_____
_____
_____

What are some of the ways in which you practice good listening?

_____
_____
_____
_____
_____

Any other thoughts on listening?

_____
_____
_____
_____
_____

My challenge to you

Now that you have given this topic some thought, here is my challenge to you:

No matter where you are on the listening spectrum, I'm sure you could agree there is room for improvement. We owe this to ourselves and, more importantly, to those around us. People love us for many reasons, but as one journal response states, "Listening is the highest form of loving."

I would like you to try this exercise daily for a month. I'm sure you might not get a chance every day, but find a conversation and apply this strategy:

Sit with a person or listen intently on the phone with all that you have. Just listen to each word; do not start thinking of a response. There will be time for that if they want it. But your job right now in that conversation is to really listen. Be curious, not bored. Get rid of any distractions. Turn away from what you are doing and any electronic distractions. You want to give this person 100% of your attention.

As they are talking, look them in the eye. Don't let your eyes wander. Nod your head in response so that they know you are listening. Resist the temptation to think of how you can help them. Also resist trying to think what you are going to say. If they say something that you missed, or think is important, ask them to repeat what they just said. Make sure you understand their perspective. Your opinions, your judgments, your solutions to their dilemma do not matter right now. There is time for that if they want it.

When they are done—and let silence determine when they are done—you can do a few things. You can repeat back what you think you heard. Again, you're not looking for more information for your answer, but helping them get clarity on what they are saying. Sometimes that's all they need. Make them feel you are truly interested.

You can (and maybe should) also ask some questions so you can understand more about their issue. The goal here is to really try and understand where they are coming from. Do they have pain and need healing? Are they struggling with someone or something?

Then, and only then, should you ask if they want your opinion, or some suggestions. But honestly, it's almost better to end your comments with a heartfelt thank you. Let them know you are grateful they are comfortable sharing things like this with you. Let them know you are always there for them.

And if it's a light conversation you might be having with your spouse or partner, try practicing the same technique. I know for me in the morning, Jody and I have coffee everyday checking in with each other and Jody might have some stories to share. I am her partner, and this is part of my responsibility to her to be a great listener. Even if I might have heard a similar version of the story the day before, I need to be patient and listen. I need to let her tell me what she wants to tell me. It's a form of love that we all need to practice.

Let's all commit to working on this most important life skill. When you improve this skill and put it to use, your relationships will flourish, and people will love you more as you begin to get better at listening.

CHAPTER 9

VULNERABILITY

Vulnerability is, in my opinion, the second most important virtue to develop healthy long-lasting relationships that stand the test of time and go way beyond casual friendship. And for so many people, especially men, they spend their life avoiding it when in fact their life would be better if they did it more.

First, you must learn to understand what being vulnerable is and what it can do for you and your close friends. As you will see from the journal comments in this chapter, many men think of it as a weakness. I myself was brought up that way. But it is one of the greatest strengths that you can build for yourself.

When you put on your armor each morning and prepare for your day, you are preventing others from knowing what you need, what you want, how you feel, and how they can help you in certain situations. When you wear this armor, you can seem aloof, not interested, shallow, and without a soul. People who care, people that you want in your life, reach you easier and quicker when you are vulnerable.

I'm not suggesting you run around and just tell people what you need. Listen first to their needs. Build rapport, then open up and share your innermost feelings. It will backfire at times, and you may feel judgment and criticism from others. In those moments, it's time to question if these are the people you want in your life.

My story

As I sat at the kitchen table looking him straight in the eye, I tried as hard as I could to summon the compassion, the courage, and the words to let my father know how much he was hurting me, my wife, and my children with his behavior.

As the words flowed from my mouth, I could see the anger, the disappointment in me, and the defense mechanisms kick in. He lashed out for what seemed like five minutes. How ungrateful I am, how I am dishonoring him, how outrageous I was being in my accusations. When he finally finished, I let silence fill the room. I just stared at him.

"Dad, I love you more than anyone on this planet. You have done so much for me, and I am overwhelmed with gratitude for everything you have done for me over my entire life. Working with you in the family business has been the best work experience ever. All that you taught me as a young man and now as a partner in the business has helped guide me and mentor me like no other."

His red face and scowl seemed to melt away. He was always searching for accolades, handwritten notes of thanks, reassurance that I knew he was always there for me.

I began speaking again in the kindest loving way I could. But I needed to be brutally honest without fear of losing my position in the firm, without fear of being judged again by his ranting voice, and with the full knowledge I was taking a huge risk.

His drinking had become so prevalent, he was talking to my young sons in an inappropriate way. They were easily influenced by my father as they loved him. They did not know that his inappropriate and offensive language was wrong and I needed to protect them from my father's behavior.

He listened and did not interrupt as I spoke softly, in a kind tone that seemed to resonate a little as tears filled his eyes. I suggested again that he get help. He softly said that maybe this was the message he needed to hear to stop drinking, and that he would stop that day. This was a good sign that he knew he needed help, and he knew that damage he was doing to our family.

But he was so independent, and he wanted to continue feeling that he could do anything on his own. *"I am a Marine and I have the strength to do this, I do not need any help."* This was not the first time we had this conversation and not the first time he promised to quit, so I knew it would not work. He needed an intervention, as well as formal rehab, and that was going to be a big push for both our family and for him.

We talked a bit more and I thanked him for listening to me. But then I needed to give him the message I came to deliver; that I was going to prevent him from seeing my boys until he got professional help and worked on his behavior with all of us. I told him Mom could still see them, but we would not be coming here until he has worked on himself. The anger in him showed up again, and the guilt I felt for the pain I was causing him and my mom really hit me. I told him again I loved both of them unconditionally, but this was going to happen. I will still see him at work, and I would also stop by once in a while to grab early coffee with him and my mom. That was always a special thing we had with each other.

Thus began a seven-month time in my life that was sad, stressful, and, in a way, shameful for what my dad was going through. I felt at least somewhat responsible for his grief. We had additional chats during that time and even came close to a family intervention, but he continued to drink in excess for the rest of his life. And unfortunately, that's what killed him in the end.

Before he passed, over time I brought my kids back into his life, but it was never the same. As they grew, they realized why my dad was the way he was, and they found ways to continue loving him despite his controlling and alcoholic behaviors.

Being vulnerable is probably one of the hardest things for a human to do. It does not come naturally, so it takes contemplated effort. Our flight-or-fight instincts usually take over immediately, and we put up our guard when our vulnerability becomes known. The fear we sense is real, and we automatically try to protect ourselves. There is a misconception that being vulnerable is a sign of weakness. Men, especially, have a hard time being vulnerable because we do not want to look weak, especially in front of other men. But in fact, it takes courage and strength to be vulnerable. And by being vulnerable, you let people know more of the "real you," which can open and deepen relationships better than trying to hold up facades. Vulnerability is not so much a sign of being weak, rather it's a sign *that you know your weakness*. And that's actually a strength, because now you can work on it.

I have worked very hard on this in my life. Especially in more recent years, but probably because I'm so much more aware of it. I believe that the inability to be vulnerable is part of the reason why my first marriage failed. With Jody, I work through the resistance every day and now can safely say I am much better at it. It's hard, but I am so glad that I pursue this challenge.

We all have our own personal collection of fears, flaws, insecurities, and weaknesses. That doesn't make us "men." That makes us "humans." But if left unchecked, those things can also hold us back in the relationships we want to continue nurturing in our lives.

What do others have to say?

Here are some important questions with actual responses from other men like you:

What is the first thing that comes to mind when you think of the word "vulnerable"?

"The first thing that comes to mind when I think of the word 'vulnerable' is the word 'naive.' To me, vulnerability represents being unaware, weak, somebody easily taken for granted."

Charles W.

"Vulnerability makes me think about how I grew up hearing from my dad, 'Stop crying or I'll give you something to cry about.'"

Seth S.

"As someone who likes to be in control, vulnerability is hard for me. I believe it means setting up a situation where you agree to give someone else some degree of power over you. To me, that is the ultimate affirmation of trust and love. I am not talking about crying when watching a movie. It's too much work to try to hide emotions like that."

Anonymous

"Being vulnerable is the practiced art of letting people know how human you are, how fragile you are, while you're working on building inner strength."

Roger L.

"The first thing that comes to mind when I think of vulnerability is drawing people in."

Vincent B.

How has a time when you experienced being vulnerable helped you change in some way?

"The first time I opened up to casual friends about needing pharmacological and talk therapy was pretty liberating. It really made the need for such therapy more acceptable to me by simply voicing it and by seeing how little anyone gave a shit. And, of course, you learn how many fellow travelers there are out there. The risk I perceived in coming out that way has been more than rewarded. And it gave me a ton more empathy for those who suffer their own different types of mental health challenges."

Ken F.

"Exposing and asking for help with my alcoholism 32 years ago required me to be vulnerable, and being vulnerable allowed others to step in and provide the help I needed."

Tim H.

Is it difficult for you to open up and ask for what you need, to talk about how you are feeling, or to have the hard conversations? If so, why do you think those things are hard for you?

"Actually, over the years this has become easier. As I am in my 60s now, I believe all of my life experiences have given me the perspective to open up and be willing to be more vulnerable."

Anonymous

"Yes, it is very difficult for me to open up and express my feelings fully with anyone. I think the reason is I don't want people to think I'm a weak and vulnerable person."

Anonymous

"It's not hard to think about what I need, but when I feel that saying it out loud would change nothing, then it's too easy to bury it."

Roger L.

"This has always been difficult as I am afraid people will see me as needy and weak. I have never loved myself enough to imagine that anyone else could possibly love me too."

Tim H.

Any other thoughts on being vulnerable?

"This is a difficult topic. I think that open and honest conversations help us move forward and make improvements."

Brent K.

"It makes me uncomfortable to think about being vulnerable!"

Anonymous

"Being vulnerable is not a bad thing. It enables you to adapt to situations and be better for it. Life is a long journey, and it requires significant ability to change to live a healthy life."

Keith D.

"I like the 'at risk' concept because it immediately suggests there's a reward to be gained in vulnerability. Just as there is no free lunch in life, there is no reward without risk. The corollary is that taking risk—in this context, making yourself vulnerable to a potentially bad outcome—almost always has a reward."

Ken F.

Your Turn:

If you want the best results possible from this book, answer the journaling questions before moving onto the next section.

What is the first thing that comes to mind when you think of the word "vulnerable"?

_____
_____
_____
_____

How has a time when you experienced being vulnerable helped you change in some way?

_____
_____
_____
_____
_____

Is it difficult for you to open up and ask what you need, to talk about how you are feeling, or to have the hard conversations? If so, why do you think those things are hard for you?

_____
_____
_____
_____
_____

Any other thoughts on being vulnerable?

_____
_____
_____

My challenge to you

Now that you have given this topic some thought, here is my challenge to you:

Being vulnerable is hard and, frankly, in my opinion, even harder for men. Perhaps that is evident in this chapter's journal responses. But you can also see that we all know we are better off learning ways to practice and embrace this most important trait.

I think it begins with a self-assessment of ourselves.

- ☐ Do we believe we are good humans?
- ☐ Are we loving, kind, thoughtful, and caring?
- ☐ Do we believe that we have parts of us that might need work?
- ☐ Do we have things we are hiding and not being open and honest about?

I do, and I'm sure you do too to some extent. All of this makes up our authentic self. All the good, the bad, and the ugly. People want to know the real and authentic you, so start thinking about how you can do that.

Find a person you trust, a person who cares about you as much as you care about them. Have them read this chapter and ask them if they would be willing to have an open, honest, and confidential chat to discuss this topic.

It won't be easy, and I can't guarantee the outcome will be positive. But what I do know is that you will begin the process of learning to be vulnerable. Once you chat with this person, move onto others. Magic will begin to happen. You will love those around you more and they will love you more as you both begin to be more vulnerable.

I always try to find friends that I can be vulnerable with. And I don't completely open up 100% on day one. It's a process of talking, listening, and building trust. Go slow but give it a try. You might be surprised how your life will change for the better.

Here are some other ways to work on your vulnerability muscle:

- Each day, check in with yourself and identify your emotional state (ex. Happy, sad, stressed, lonely, anxious).
- Honor that emotional state by telling someone else (ex. spouse, partner or friend).
- Discern what, if anything, needs to be learned.
- Each week, reflect on a difficult conversation that needs to happen. Challenge yourself to have that conversation with someone.

CHAPTER 10

HUMILITY

At the core of humility is the idea that we all have gifts and talents, as well as imperfections. We use our gifts to help ourselves become successful; to do well in our career, to build a successful business, to build relationships, to write books, to speak in public, to coach individuals, or whatever success means for you. At the same time, as humans we have flaws and insecurities, and it's the existence of both talents and gifts, and our imperfections, that make us human. When we fully understand this concept, we can begin to let down our guard a bit and become comfortable in our own skin. We learn to be open to criticism from others and begin to realize that we do not have all the answers. This can be a huge growth moment for all of us.

The key to living a humble life is to recognize our strengths, but not let them make us believe we are superior to others. And at the same time, not let our imperfections become the focus of who we are, and allow that focus devalue ourselves. When we can balance our gifts and talents with the notion that we are human and have flaws like everyone else, we can become humble and live a successful happy life.

Humility is one of those virtues that is often developed in yourself over a long period of time, with lots of reflection and practice. Regardless of how you were influenced growing up, you might find humility to be difficult. For example, if you have an overbearing sense of self-worth, and do not take time to recognize the contributions of others, you will struggle with being humble. Maybe you feel you are superior to others, which may lead to you having a hard time admitting when you're wrong or accepting feedback.

If you have a hard time being vulnerable and open to sharing your weaknesses, you may not come across as being humble, but rather better than everyone else. I'm sure you can think of people in your life that always think they are right, rarely admit they are wrong, and have an inflated sense of themselves. They also tend to be competitive and lack perspective, and they may be insecure; so they find it hard to be humble.

As you read this chapter, I want you to begin a process of self-awareness to see where you are on the spectrum. You will have your chance at the end to do the journaling questions, but have an open mind when you think of yourself. This book is about evolving, and this is a great area to spend time working on yourself.

My story

"You are not doing a very good job marketing yourself or your company." Nancy said that to me over lunch one day as she was trying to convince me that I should hire her to do public relations for our firm. It was an uncomfortable feeling to have this outgoing, smart, and successful person telling me all the things we should be doing. She could tell I was feeling awkward and changed tactics.

She started asking me pointed questions about my sales process, the history of our fourth-generation firm, and my personal goals and aspirations. As I began to speak, describing a litany of success that we have achieved over the years, she was surprised none of this was in our marketing material. She could not understand why we were not making a bigger deal of our success or the value we bring to our clients.

Then she described all the things that I need to do to promote myself and my company to get to the next level. Write articles for the local business journal and make sure I include a photo of myself. Build a self-promotion marketing campaign that included full page ads in trade publications with large photos of me and my brother, Chuck. Gather testimonials from clients. Get them to say how great we were. The list went on.

At this point I just wanted to end the lunch. I told Nancy straight out that this was just not something I could do, nor did I want to do it.

I suppose a lot of this lack of self-promotion came from the culture of our company which was led by my father. He and my mom made sure our family knew that we were not braggers. "There is no need to brag about your accomplishments, let them speak for themselves." Growing up with this culture influenced how I lived my life and how I conducted business.

There were many competitors and other successful business leaders that I knew of that did a great job self-promoting. But some were aggressive and that to me always looked distasteful.

As lunch was winding down, Nancy suggested I read a book that she recommends to all her clients. It was probably the best business advice that anyone ever gave me, as it changed the direction of my life.

I went to the bookstore that afternoon and there it was. *Brag!: The Art of Tooting Your Own Horn without Blowing It,* by Peggy Klaus. I began reading it that night and there was a quiet calm that came over me as I began to be convinced that it was okay to live a humble life but also let others know how you can help them. It has never been, "Hey, look at me!" That book taught me how to self-promote without feeling like a bragger.

Living a life with humility is hard. As my career went along and my stature and visibility grew in the business community, I had to balance this success with the ability to always remember where I came from and where I started. Our company grew, our image went far and wide, but we always felt grounded in our core values. Our parents influenced us to be good people. Humility is grounded in many of the other virtues written about in this book. They are all tightly woven together and, as you will see below, not everyone has figured out the right balance. But they all know that humility is important as a life virtue.

What do others have to say?

Here are some important questions with actual responses from other men like you:

What does being humble mean to you? Do you feel you are a humble person, or that you need to work on this skill?

"Humility is, to me, about service to others. Truly focusing on others versus myself. At my core I believe I am a humble person. That said, I clearly have times where I find myself being arrogant, vain, or self-serving. Absolutely I still need to work at being humble. Most importantly, I find I am happier when I am humble and I don't like myself when I'm not."

Anonymous

"The essence of being humble is treating people like equals, independent of social status, education, or financial condition. I do feel I am a humble person, but this is a skill that we must always be vigilant about and work on."

Robert W.

The opposite of humility is acting with selfish behaviors, arrogance, or vanity. Think of a time when you were acting without humility. Or, in other words, you were the focus, and the outcome was all about building yourself up, even at the cost of those around you. How did it make you feel? What was the outcome? If you don't have a story about you, share one about someone in your life and how it affected you.

"I enjoy my financial success much more than my father ever did. At one point in my career, I purchased a top-of-the-line Jaguar automobile. It was the most beautiful car I ever owned. I lost two decent customers who noticed the car and felt I was 'overcharging them.' I honestly could hear my dad in heaven telling me what a fool I was! From the day I traded it in, I drive a nice car, but a vehicle of 'the people' so that I never stand out again."

Charles P.

"I was the managing partner in my business for 13 years before I got the actual title as CEO when my partner retired. Absolutely nothing about my job changed. I still was leading the company just like I had those many years before. But, once I had the title as CEO, I became very full of myself. I found myself wanting to make sure everyone now knew that I was the CEO. Fortunately, I had a great friend who called me out on this. He knew me intimately before I had the title and saw the ugly transformation once I had it. Thankfully, with his guidance I was able to pivot back to being a better 'servant leader' who, for 13 years, didn't need a title to be a good leader. Once again, I realized I liked myself better and was significantly more effective as a servant leader versus an arrogant CEO who was full of himself."

Anonymous

Any other thoughts on humility?

"It is the opposite of weakness and shows the strength of one's inner self-confidence."

Joseph A.

"I'm not a psychologist, but I see two forms of humility. One is born of confidence and is the strong form. Humility with confidence is a powerful way to live and you can feel it in those who have it. The other comes from lack of confidence and holds people back because it comes from having a low view of oneself. The second can be destructive over time."

Ken F.

"Humble people are always the most interesting people to be around. They are confident without being arrogant. They want to realize their gifts and help others do the same."

Carter V.

Your Turn:

If you want the best results possible from this book, answer the journaling questions before moving onto the next section.

What does being humble mean to you? Do you feel you are a humble person or that you need to work on this skill?

_____
_____
_____
_____

The opposite of humility is acting with selfish behaviors, arrogance, or vanity. Think of a time when you were acting without humility. Or in other words you were the focus, and the outcome was all about building yourself up rather than those around you, at any cost. Write the story and how it made you feel. What was the outcome? If you don't have a story about you, share one about someone in your life and how it affected you.

_____
_____
_____
_____

If one of your friends, family members, or teammates came to you for help on how to be humbler, what would you tell them?

_____
_____
_____

Any other thoughts on humility?

_____
_____
_____

My challenge to you

Now that you have given this topic some thought, here is my challenge to you:

When I think of humility, people like Mother Theresa and Mahatma Gandhi come to mind. They spent their lives working with some of the poorest populations on our planet. And I also think of many of the men who contributed to this book who have made it clear they fully understand this concept and live their lives with a sense of humility.

I don't think we spend enough time talking or thinking about this idea of being humble. It takes some inward thinking on what your behavior and responses are around your friends. If many of your friends are not humble, then that behavior will spill over onto you. There is comfort in emulating close friends. Changing your behavior without a supportive network of friends who are on the same path is difficult.

As you journal through these questions, also take time to have some discussion with friends who you feel are humble. Ask them some of these journaling questions. Speak to your spouse or partner about this. If you have children, ask them what they think. There is also plenty of additional material available to read on this topic.

Embracing humility is a lifelong journey. I work on this every day and am always self-reflecting on how I can do better. I want the same for you. So, I want you to try the following in your journal. Write down and answer these questions:

- Am I a humble person? Am I being truly honest with myself on this?
- What are my talents and my imperfections? Make a list of all of your strengths and weaknesses. Be honest with yourself about what you are good at and where you can make improvements. This awareness will help you become more humble.
- Am I a good listener? Practice active listening, which means really listening to what the other person is saying and not focusing on your response.
- Am I good at seeking and receiving feedback? It is a good practice to find others who can give you feedback to help you uncover blind spots in your behavior that you might not be aware of. Use the feedback you receive to make changes in your attitude and behavior so that you become more humble.

Some other suggestions for learning to be humbler.

- Cultivate gratitude. Make sure you are expressing gratitude to others on a regular basis. You owe a lot to those that have helped you along your life journey; let them know you appreciate them.
- Practice Empathy. Are you willing and able to put yourself in other peoples' shoes and truly understand their perspective? Being able to do this will broaden your understanding of how things really are and what some new possibilities are for you.
- One of the best places to practice humility can be found in serving others. Finding an organization that has opportunities to volunteer will give you a chance to help someone who really needs help. Think of serving in shelters or food banks, or even mentoring someone who could use some coaching to improve their life.

CHAPTER 11

FORGIVENESS

I get that you might not be a forgiving person. The act of forgiving is learned during our younger years and is influenced by personal experience, values, and beliefs. Some people struggle with this idea of forgiving others as you will see in the men's comments below. But it is something that can be learned and practiced as you go through life. I think forgiveness is also influenced by the severity and nature of the offense. This is an important virtue and I want you to read this chapter carefully and then spend some time with the challenge at the end.

But right now, I want you to think a little bit about what is going on when you feel like you can't forgive someone. It weighs on your mind and is ever present, especially when that person is in your presence or their name is mentioned. Instantly, the memory of the action is in the forefront of your mind and you become agitated, and sometimes outright angry. The other person may not ever think about it, as if it's over, and they may not even know they harmed you because you may never have said anything to the person and you just carry this emotion around with you like a heavy suitcase.

When you hold onto this grudge, you are harboring feelings of resentment, anger, and bitterness towards this person for something that took place in the past. Something that you cannot change. It happened and it's over. When you can't forgive, you end up reliving the past offense over and over in your mind and carrying around these negative emotions. This can have a detrimental effect on your emotional wellbeing, your relationships, and your personal growth.

On the other hand, when you take some steps to reconcile with that person—or even reconcile in your own mind—you open up room for a happier, less stressful life. When you learn to forgive, you begin the process of healing by letting go of negative emotions, letting go of the grudge, and opening up the opportunity for personal growth.

Forgiveness is an intentional act on your part to accept the offense, release resentment, and work towards peace with yourself and possibly restoring the relationship with the person who caused the harm.

I want you to read this chapter with an open mind and an open heart. Don't be stubborn and hold back a chance to evolve. It's 100% on you to make the decision to forgive. Sit for a minute and imagine your life with no grudge. With that burden lifted, you would have more room for love in your heart, more space to deepen those relationships you really care about, and energy to put towards happier times.

My story

It was late in the day on Friday, it had been a long week, and I was having a coffee in my office when in walked one of our most dedicated teammates. She asked if I had a minute and if she could talk to me. As she entered, she shut the door behind her, which was highly unusual.

She sat across from me in one of the chairs facing my desk. It was a small office, so she was very close. I saw that she had tears in her eyes and as I tried to prepare for what might be coming next, my mind raced so hard I barely heard her first words.

"I need to tell you something that I'm not supposed to know, and neither are you, but I feel compelled to tell you. You cannot let anyone know it was me that told you, you will find out anyway soon."

Now I had more confusion, wondering what the hell she was leading up to. Then, this:

"Gene, George, Peter, and Tommy are leaving our company. They started a competing firm and today is their last day. They are planning on coming in tomorrow to grab some things and move into their new office Monday."

It was hard to believe that these four business colleagues, who I called close friends, would even think about leaving our company and starting a competing business. What was even harder is that they did it behind our backs and had been scheming for months to make their exit. They had office space, stationary, business cards, phones, the works. They were a legit business and overnight they were gone.

Our company was smaller back then, so this exit had an impact on our finances, on our reputation, and on our future. At first, emotions like anger, frustration, concern, and anxiety filled our company and spread like wildfire. George, Gene, Peter, and Tom all had books of business that, in total, amounted to about 20% of our revenue. For me it wasn't about the money, it was about my relationships with them personally. Some of them were at my wedding, one of them was a childhood friend who I mentored into the business, another was a young man who I also mentored into the business and helped become a successful salesperson.

I took it personally. I was hurt, embarrassed, and questioning my role as a leader, mentor, and human being. Had I pushed them out? What could I have done differently? Who else in the company might join them? What would everyone in the business community think about us going forward? It became more about me and less about them.

My dad was furious. Sure, he was hurt, but his emotions turned into vengeance, anger, and a mission to shut them down and put them out of business. It became a decade-long battle for him, and I could tell he could not let it go, and frankly he took it so badly that I think this notched up his drinking even more at a time when he was already drinking every day.

I reached out to all of them one at a time. Some called back, some did not. They felt it was important to take a try at running their own business. The lawsuits began to fly around as they violated their non-compete contracts. A cease and desist order was put in place, but over time all their clients followed them because the laws around covenant not to compete are hard to enforce.

After a deep dive on their business and the 20% of revenue they took with them, I came to realize those particular clients had a high cost to service, were a huge drain on our staff, and was overall not the kind of business that our company was really interested in writing.

This shift in thinking for me was the beginning of some soul searching and got me on a path of forgiveness. Yes, it hurt. Yes, I was ashamed and embarrassed. And yes, I wish they had not left, because I lost four good friends. Seeing them at some local insurance functions was hard. Getting calls from clients who decided to move their business was painful. But, after about six months, we realized that our company was going to be okay. And there was plenty of room in our regional business area for many more insurance brokers. The loss hardened my dad, but it began to soften me. I had no control over what they decided to do. Frankly, it was history now and we had to come to terms with the business side of things. We had a team of 25 people that depended on us to keep going, and we did.

I dug deep and reframed what had happened. They had every right to leave and start their own company. It's the American dream. We were fine, so why cling onto this pain and frustration? I began to forgive them. This change in me manifested itself into an overall forgiveness for everyone in my life. It felt like a heavy load was being lifted from my heart and soul. I had to stay away from this conversation with my dad as he held onto his anger, rage, and desire for revenge. I realized how much pain this was causing him and how, parallel to that, nothing in his life changed.

I am now in a state of total forgiveness for all sins. Mine included. I have made mistakes, I have hurt people, and I have made amends. But this does not come easily for others, and I respect that. As a matter of fact, Jody leans more towards not forgiving as quickly. Yet we coexist and have a loving, kind relationship. And we have forgiven each other for any hurt we may have caused each other.

As I read the responses for this chapter's journal questions, I felt that many men used this reflection to write about things they were sorry for and about people they need to forgive, especially now that they are aging. Many mentioned how alcohol played a role in ruining relationships and had made amends to those people by asking for forgiveness. I got the overall feeling that when it's time to ask for forgiveness, that comes easier than giving forgiveness.

What do others have to say?

Here are some important questions with actual responses from other men like you:

What is your experience with forgiveness? What have you forgiven and why?

"Every time I have forgiven someone—or, more importantly, asked for forgiveness—I have experienced great peace. In most cases it leads to a healing between us. For example, my father and I had a challenging relationship. For many years we had an on-and-off relationship. More times off than on. On Father's Day two years before he passed, I went over to meet with him. We healed immediately. During the last year of his life, I was his best friend and soulmate. For that I am forever blessed."

Anonymous

"My experience is that when you forgive someone you really free yourself. When you hold on to the anger, hurt, and resentment, the person you need to forgive lives rent free in your mind. The anger festers, and bubbles up from time to time and disturbs your ability to enjoy your day. They might not even know that you are angry with them so they are going on with their life as if nothing ever happened."

John B.

"I've forgiven myself for past decisions, which has freed me from any regret though not necessarily some sadness. That's been relatively easy for me in my adult life. As a younger adult I was faster to judge and not forgive others, being tied up in a fealty to certain principles and not being able to consider other factors that may have contributed to another's actions."

David S.

Are there people you have yet to forgive, or will never forgive? Why is that?

"Right now, I'm having trouble forgiving my sisters for not doing more to support our mother who is 92 and not in good shape. As long as they choose to not support her, I might find it difficult to be alright with it. At the same time, there's another part of me that is telling me that life is too short to be angry with others—which I truly believe. That feeling has helped me reduce my frustration with this situation."

David S.

"Yes, when I started my company, I was sued by my previous employer who alleged I had stolen trade secrets (which I hadn't). An individual at the company made statements under oath that were not true. This could have potentially ended my insurance career and would have had a huge negative impact on my family. Subsequently, this individual tried to make amends and while I was always cordial, I have never forgiven him."

Jeffrey C.

What are the benefits or detriments of forgiving? For yourself, for the other person, for the community?

"Some benefits of forgiveness; it can inspire change for the better from the person in need of forgiveness, and it can strengthen relationships. It is easier to forgive and move on than to be weighed down by grudges."

Keith B.

"Forgiving someone is something you should do for yourself. It frees your soul. The detriments of forgiving only happen when you are not sincere when you forgive someone. This only causes you to continue to feel the anger and pretend what happened does not bother you. You need to deal with the issue and make sure the forgiveness is real."

John B.

"Withholding forgiveness is living in the past. Life is too short to carry that burden. It is so much better to forgive and move forward. Focus on the future and not the past. A good lesson for a world so full of hatred."

Michael L.

Any other thoughts on forgiveness?

"Forgiveness doesn't wipe away all hurt and pain, but it does move you closer towards healing, in my opinion."

Brent K.

"Forgiveness does not mean that someone gets a free pass for bad behavior. Sometimes, forgiving someone can be the end of a chapter or relationship. The forgiver must decide whether or not the person they're forgiving is someone who they want to continue being involved with. Sometimes it is best to move on."

Noah E.

"Looked at from the other side, it is important to apologize if you have done something wrong that affects others. 'I'm sorry' is one of the most powerful phrases in any language."

Jeffrey C.

Your Turn:

If you want the best results possible from this book, answer the journaling questions before moving onto the next section.

What is your experience with forgiveness? What have you forgiven and why?

_____
_____
_____
_____
_____

Are there people you have yet to forgive, or will never forgive? Why is that?

_____
_____
_____
_____
_____

What are the benefits or detriments of forgiving? For yourself, for the other person, for the community?

_____
_____
_____
_____
_____

Any other thoughts on forgiveness?

_____
_____
_____

My challenge to you

Now that you have given this topic some thought, here is my challenge to you:

As you begin to think about your relationship with forgiveness, first get clear on where you are. Talk to others in an open and vulnerable way. There is no right or wrong here as you can see from the journal responses. But there is a common thread that being more forgiving does allow for more peace in your own mind. So maybe moving in that direction would change part of who you are in a better way.

Perhaps forgiving yourself for your past transgressions is a start. We can all do that. Then, maybe think of some people in your life that have caused you harm that you can forgive, and let that hurt go from your heart. It may be hard, but it is possible.

I know you have been hurt in ways that are hard to even think about. Family, friends, business partners, and complete strangers may have caused you unbearable harm and pain. And those memories are etched into you like a tattoo on your arm. Covering it up with a long sleeve shirt does not make it go away. Close your eyes and picture the person who you cannot forgive. Look at them and feel their presence. Do they even know what they did to hurt you? Do they lose sleep over the action or lack of action? If you take a small step towards forgiving that person, you will begin to heal. Your heart will erase the pain that you carry and make room for more love and gratitude for the life that you live today.

Some final questions to think about

- ☐ How does my relationship with forgiveness serve me in my life today?
- ☐ Do I need to think about a different vantage point?
- ☐ Will learning to be more forgiving assist me in my life and relationships?

CHAPTER 12

REGRETS

My relationship with regrets has changed over the years. I remember in both my personal and business life, I spent countless hours ruminating over my past actions, wishing I had done things differently, wondering what my life would be like if I had behaved and acted in a different way. It can be as small as something I said to a big thing like my first marriage that failed.

These feelings of regret can take over your mind, consume your day, and fill you with negative energy. You begin to beat yourself up, and this all has a negative effect on your health, relationships, and ability to see clearly. Your self-confidence can fade and you begin to doubt yourself.

This is not a way to live. We all make mistakes that we wish we could take back. The reality is that you cannot take anything back. But you can make amends with people by apologizing and you can start looking at regret as a learning experience.

My story

The $10 bill was sticking up out of the paper dixie cup on the shelf just above the washing machine. Our basement was always dark, so it was not easy to see, but I saw it. This is where my mom put any change she found in our clothes when she did our laundry.

As a 10-year-old, with a passion to build things—especially models—this was enough money to get the next AURA model that I recently saw at the hobby shop, which was only a bicycle ride away from my house. I looked around as if someone might be there watching me and when I felt like the coast was clear, I carefully took the $10 bill from the cup while making sure I did not disturb any of the other smaller bills.

I ran upstairs past my mom with a bounce in my step and headed to my bedroom to get whatever money I had saved from doing chores around the house so I could head out and buy the new model. As I ran past my mom again, she asked where I was going and I said the model shop, I would be right back. She gave me a kiss and a hug and off I went.

Cruising the aisles with a pocket full of cash always gave me some confidence that my hard work around the house had its benefits. Having my own money was important to my wellbeing and independence as a person. "Hard work does pay off," was a lesson my dad taught me at a young age.

That afternoon, I spent about three hours prepping this new model. It was a replica of an older Jeep CJ5, and I was going to customize it and enter the monthly model contest. Every part was removed, organized, and cleaned up as needed. I read through the instructions to make sure I had all the paint I needed and any other extra parts like wire, extra tires, material for a custom roof rack, and lights. I was in my element with this new purchase.

At dinner that night, my mom asked me how I did with the new model. My dad praised me for doing the chores and having the money to buy it on my own. A small shred of guilt crept in about me taking the $10, but I was confident that my mom would never notice.

Family dinners were always important to us and a time to chat about each of our days and see if there might be a family TV show to watch later.

Everything was going fine until my mom asked straight up if anyone took a $10 bill out of her money cup in the laundry room. She had just put it there that morning, so she knew it was there.

It was not my dad for sure, so Susan, Chuck, and I looked at each other. They both said no, they did not take it, which left me with the decision on whether to lie or tell the truth. All eyes were on me as my face began to turn bright red and I was about to cry having been caught. "Was it you honey?" my mom asked. Embarrassed and scared, I said that I took it, and I was going to tell her I just forgot. She said I had plenty of time during the day and she was surprised that I took it without telling her. Then the heavy parenting came out. "I'm very disappointed," said my dad. Always the worst thing to hear from a parent. After more lecturing directed at the three of us, we were excused. No TV for me that night!

This memory has stayed with me my entire life and, over the years, I have talked to my mom about it more than my dad. And while I still feel bad that I did it, I learned a huge life lesson. And that is how I carry this moment around. Because of this, I do not lie, cheat, or steal. Certainly, those are things we are taught at a young age anyway, but this experience solidified that teaching for me.

We can look back over our lives and pinpoint many times when we could have done things differently, hoping for a different outcome, but we can't go back and change what we did or the decision we made. We sometimes focus on these regrets instead of focusing on all the positive things that have happened in our lives.

What do others have to say?

Here are some important questions with actual responses from other men like you:

How does regret affect you, and has this changed over time?

"Forgiveness doesn't wipe away all hurt and pain, but it does move you closer towards healing, in my opinion."

Brent K.

"Forgiveness does not mean that someone gets a free pass for bad behavior. Sometimes, forgiving someone can be the end of a chapter or relationship. The forgiver must decide whether or not the person they're forgiving is someone who they want to continue being involved with. Sometimes it is best to move on."

Noah E.

"Looked at from the other side, it is important to apologize if you have done something wrong that affects others. 'I'm sorry' is one of the most powerful phrases in any language."

Jeffrey C.

At times when you felt regret, what did you do to try and work through those feelings?

"Any time I feel regretful, I sit with the feeling until I understand why I feel that way. This is the gateway to a solution or a lesson. When those feelings are regarding an event or occasion that I can no longer control or change, then I forgive myself for my part in the regretful activity and move forward with the lesson, committing to doing it differently next time."

Stew D.

"Prayer is important. Prayer helps frame self-reflection, which is critical. Besides prayer, I identify the mistakes, apologize often, and reiterate how important anyone I might have hurt is to me."

Michael L.

"I prefer to ask myself questions and try to seek for learning opportunities rather than focusing on the past and what could have been. I ask questions like, 'What can I do going forward?' and, 'What can I learn from this?'"

Vincent B.

If you take a moment to think of past regrets as opportunities to learn, what are some of those lessons?

"My top three common regrets are (a) I wish I'd spent more time with that person (especially before they passed away or moved away), (b) I wish I hadn't reacted emotionally in a certain way that negatively affected a person, and (c) I wish I'd severed a relationship earlier because it was a big-time waste for both of us. So, the lessons from those regrets influence my behavior moving forward."

Chip C.

"One lesson I have embodied is being more receptive to people whose relationship I might now have prioritized in the past. Another is being a better listener and receptive to trying new things."

Greg C.

"The only regret that was hard to battle was my marriage. What could I have done differently, why did I not seek a better work-life balance, why could I not make my marriage work. My decision to get divorced was the toughest in my life but was also the best decision in my life. I often reflect on my behavior while married to ensure I avoid making the same mistakes again in my new relationships. Especially understanding my personality better and letting things go that are not really important. Also trying to better listen to my partner's point of view and understand what is driving it."

Joseph A.

Any other thoughts on regret?

"While not frequent, alcohol has played a part in about 25% of my regrettable actions; mainly from my younger years."

Rino P.

"Every one of us carries some form of regret for something. To ignore or not acknowledge that we truly have regrets is a missed opportunity to hone ourselves into someone more mindful and caring."

Phillip E.

"Regrets are inherently neutral, and being able to express sadness and disappointment is healthy, vulnerable, and powerful."

Christopher R.

Your Turn:

If you want the best results possible from this book, answer the journaling questions before moving onto the next section.

How does regret affect you, and has this changed over time?

_____
_____
_____
_____
_____

At times when you felt regret, what did you do to try and work through those feelings?

_____
_____
_____
_____
_____

If you take a moment to think of past regrets as opportunities to learn, what are some of those lessons?

_____
_____
_____
_____
_____

Any other thoughts on regret?

_____
_____
_____
_____

My challenge to you

Now that you have given this topic some thought, here is my challenge to you:

We all make mistakes. The key is to not make the same mistake twice. That requires early and consistent learning, which I am sure you are familiar with.

If we take the approach that these mistakes are regrets that we carry around every day, that becomes a huge burden and a heavy way to go through life.

I used this lesson of stealing the $10 bill from my mom as a launch pad to make amends with my parents and my brother and sister, and to teach my children. The big lesson for me was not to lie or withhold information from anyone, and to not take things that don't belong to me. That lesson took place 56 years ago and now I always have a smile on my face when I think of that story. I smile because it is a good memory of learning something important. My point here is to think back on some stories in your past that you have held onto as a regret and where you are possibly holding some remorse on what happened. Our goal in this challenge will be to reframe how you are holding these stories in your heart so that you can lighten your load.

My challenge to you is to make a list of as many moments like this in your life that you consider a regret. As you look at this list, is there a way in your mind to reframe what you did and convert it into a lesson? Maybe there are people you hurt, and you need to make amends with them. Not so much to ease your burden, but perhaps to bring you closer to the person you make amends with. There is nothing wrong with this approach. Don't think too much about how things may have turned out because of that lesson, but rather how grateful you are for that moment of learning. And how beautiful your life is despite that incident that has been weighing you down.

CHAPTER 13

RELATIONSHIPS

Humans are social animals, and we thrive when we have strong and healthy relationships with other human beings. When we don't have healthy relationships, or when we have a limited number of close friends, we may find ourselves feeling lonely. You can live alone and not feel lonely, and at the same time you can live with someone (a spouse or partner) and feel lonely. I know many couples that live this way and it's hard on both parties.

As we journey through life, we end up spending a lot of time with other people. At the core is the family unit. Our mom and dad, maybe brothers and sisters, cousins, and more. These relationships are the first and most common relationships we can think of. And if we are lucky, these core family relationships are strong, healthy, and vibrant, and you always feel taken care of and loved when you are with them. Beyond that, it's up to us to find, nurture, and build relationships outside this small circle that was automatically created when we were born.

But getting along with people can be difficult. We are all so complicated and there are so many distractions such as phones, internet, and TV, that steal our time from having deep one-on-one conversations with friends and family. Feelings can get hurt, conversations can be misunderstood, and in a short time, relationships can fall by the wayside.

It is critical to get this right. The feeling of isolation and loneliness can have serious health consequences such as increased risk of heart disease, stroke, and dementia. Men in particular have a greater likelihood of feeling isolated and lonely because we have a harder time being vulnerable which can prevent us from being able to ask others what we need from them, and this prevents us from being able to deepen relationships as well. Being a good listener is also helpful when trying to open up new relationships. In summary, being vulnerable, improving your listening skills, being a bit more humble, and practicing forgiveness will all go a long way to help you make new friends and deepen existing relationships.

My story

It was 2:30 in the afternoon on Friday December 28th, 2018, and I was sitting at my desk typing a goodbye email to my 80 colleagues. It was the last day of my 38-year career and I wanted one last chance to express my gratitude and appreciation for all that we built together over the past years.

Many of my teammates had been with me for 20 years or more. Our relationships were rock solid as we had spent so much time together over a long period of time. These were my people, and I imagined all the lunches we would have and fun times gathering without the pressure of work. We could now get to know each other in a more personal way.

Before I hit send, I took one last walk around the office to say a few goodbyes to my closest colleagues. Many of them were either in a meeting, on the phone, preparing for a call, or had left the office early.

I finally hit send. As I sat there waiting for a response to my email, I realized it was time for me to leave the office. I had made sure to include my personal email for anyone to respond or stay in touch. I checked my phone over the weekend, and I could count the number of replies on one hand. Monday came and went, and still no more responses.

After a few months and a few visits to the office, I came to realize most of these relationships were situational. They existed because we worked together. The foundation for these relationships were built on common goals and aspirations. Build the business, serve our clients well, imagine and implement new strategies, improve the bottom line, and improve employee morale and engagement. All these building blocks and our success brought us closer.

When these foundational blocks disappear, what is left?

Sure, we got along great, we did amazing work together, but I had been replaced. All my clients had a new relationship manager; I had stepped down from the leadership team two years earlier, so I slowly had become irrelevant.

I noticed the same reaction from many clients. I arranged a few lunches, but quickly realized that much of our relationship was built on helping them with their insurance issues. Our conversations were more of a struggle now as we went through some personal topics and then struggled to find more to talk about.

As I began to create mine and Jody's new company, Retirement Transformed, it became clear to both of us that once you retire, you leave behind relationships that were part of your day-to-day life. It is a common struggle and change for everyone who enters this phase of life.

At the same time, I began to look at my circle of friends and family and began working hard on building and rebuilding relationships that perhaps I did not pay close enough attention to during my 38-year career. Through my research I came to realize just how critical strong, healthy relationships are to living a long fulfilling life. Humans are social animals, and we need deep healthy relationships to survive. Without them, we face a lonely life. In my opinion it is the greatest risk that retirees face and it must be paid attention to.

Jody and I continued to talk more about this; interviewing other retirees, reading multiple books, and creating online courses, all to help people to understand and have a path towards developing better relationships.

It has been nearly five years since I walked out the door of the insurance company and today, I can say that my relationships with my friends and family are better than ever. It took work, it took patience, and it took energy.

What do others have to say?

Here are some important questions with actual responses from other men like you:

How do the people with whom you share your best relationships make you feel? Do you feel supported, cared for, and seen?

"Family and close friends give me a sense of fellowship. Nothing seems to be out of bounds to discuss and have dialogue about. Some of my business client relationships also bring fulfillment to my job. Many are close friends and not just clients."

Mark K.

"The people that are my best relationships often make me feel great; loved, appreciated, respected, etcetera. But it's also more complicated; often the people that are closest to me can also disappoint, or even hurt me."

James W.

"Relationships—the right ones, of course—are energizing. They stop me from looking inward, ruminating, and worrying. They help me turn outward, look forward, and see what's possible. They also give me a sense of protection; that I have back-up for whatever adversity might come my way; that I have someone with whom to get things off my chest rather than letting them fester inside; that I have extra eyes and ears to watch out for me."

Ken F.

Do you communicate what you are looking for, or do you just expect them to know?

"I am not great at communicating what I want from people, which may be why my close relationships are so small."

Keith B.

"I do a poor job of communicating what I really want. I too often expect them to know and am disappointed when they don't provide, even when I didn't communicate."

Brent K.

Do you show up for your friends the way you want them to show up for you?

"My intentions are good, but I don't show up as well as I could. With five kids at home and running a business, my friends have been last on the list."

Brent K.

"I see a spectrum of behavior that one can have toward relationships, from reactive to proactive. I would say that I am very reliable at showing up when needed or asked to. But for years, I leaned much too far to the reactive side of the spectrum. Now, later in my life, with the maturity, confidence, and wisdom of age, I have tried to strike a better balance of being more proactive with my relationships. But that is not natural for me—it takes more work than it does for a lot of other people."

Ken F.

"Most certainly. The saying, 'Do unto others as they would do unto you' comes to mind."

David C.

If you are in a marriage or have a partner, is that the most satisfying relationship that you have? Why or why not? What does it need to get better

"My intentions are good, but I don't show up as well as I could. With five kids at home and running a business, my friends have been last on the list."

Brent K.

"I see a spectrum of behavior that one can have toward relationships, from reactive to proactive. I would say that I am very reliable at showing up when needed or asked to. But for years, I leaned much too far to the reactive side of the spectrum. Now, later in my life, with the maturity, confidence, and wisdom of age, I have tried to strike a better balance of being more proactive with my relationships. But that is not natural for me—it takes more work than it does for a lot of other people."

Ken F.

"Most certainly. The saying, 'Do unto others as they would do unto you' comes to mind."

David C.

If you are retired, how have your relationships changed? More specifically, during your career you were surrounded by dozens, if not hundreds, of colleagues, clients, and professional acquaintances. They were a huge part of your social network. What have you done to replace that network?

"Still working. Part of why I haven't hung it up. I am very dependent on my network. Perhaps a bit afraid that I won't be able to recreate the community of youth, intellectuality, curiosity and drive."

Michael L.

"I've always enjoyed my myriad of work relationships, whether it be with clients or vendors. As I approach retirement it is becoming abundantly clear to me that those relationships are almost entirely 'work based' and that they will completely disappear as soon as I'm no longer active with them. The saddest part will be losing touch with those clients/vendors with whom I was most close with, who I thought may continue to be my friends even after retirement. The more I talk with friends and acquaintances who are retired, the more I find that to be a true statement. All the more reason to nurture lasting friendships."

Phillip E.

"When I retired from full time work, I told myself I would stay in touch with colleagues who stayed in touch with me. Only a very few did, but those relationships endure to this day. When we moved, we lost touch with some friends and neighbors because we really had little to add to those relationships, but we made new friends at our new home. So, I guess I would say I have different levels of relationships. Some very enduring, some based on common interests, and some good for the current time. But I love them all knowing that to some extent, they are based on how much I am willing to contribute to the relationship."

Anonymous

Any other thoughts on relationships?

"They require work to make them work. You can't be lazy in a relationship and expect it to always remain strong."

Chuck N.

"As my father would say, 'If you are lucky, during a lifetime you will be able to count your true friends on one hand.' Focusing on those on that one hand is what's important."

Joseph A.

"Although I have nice things, I don't have much in the way of personal possessions. I don't really shop or buy things unnecessarily. The things that I do tend to collect are good, positive relationships. This is one thing I value beyond most."

Vincent B.

Your Turn:

If you want the best results possible from this book, answer the journaling questions before moving onto the next section.

How do the people with whom you share your best relationships make you feel? Do you feel supported, cared for, and seen?

_____

_____

Do you communicate what you are looking for, or do you just expect them to know?

_____

_____

Do you show up for your friends the way you want them to show up for you?

_____

_____

If you are in a marriage or have a partner, is that the most satisfying relationship that you have? Why or why not? What does it need to get better?

_____

_____

If you are retired, how have your relationships changed? More specifically, during your career you were surrounded by dozens, if not hundreds, of colleagues, clients, and professional acquaintances. They were a huge part of your social network. What have you done to replace that network?

_____

_____

Any other thoughts on relationships?

_____

_____

My challenge to you

Now that you have given this topic some thought, here is my challenge to you:

This topic is interesting, and the answers were all over the place. A few common threads are that relationships are important, they take work and cultivation, they change after retirement, and it's something we all need, especially after retirement.

The one area where I see men struggle the most is in asking close friends and family what they are looking for. And many of the responses made it clear that the men expect friends and family to know what they (the men themselves) are looking for. I believe that this inability to open up and let others know what we need from them leaves us all open to other people's interpretation of what we need.

I went deeper into this in the chapter on vulnerability. No matter how close we are to someone, it's hard to be open, honest, and vulnerable without feeling like we are needy.

It's okay to have acquaintances that are "just friends." Someone to hang with, play golf or pickleball with, or grab a meal with once in a while. But deep meaningful relationships that last for years are built on more than that.

Think of some of your closest friends, your family, or your spouse. Do you really know what they want from you in your relationship?

Make a list of your closest relationships. List out their names. Then next to each name write what you believe they need from you. Are you providing that to them? Is there more you can do to deepen your relationships?

Then, add a column on what you are currently getting from them. Is that enough? Do you wish there was more?

Start with your closest relationship, and have a conversation with them about this. It could be everything is in alignment, but then again, maybe you both are looking for more and never talked about it.

CHAPTER 14

GRATITUDE

I would imagine there are many things in your life you are grateful for. I'm sure at times you have even expressed those words out loud to someone else. We are taught at a young age to say thank you when someone does something for us. Surely you feel grateful for the roof over your head, the food on your table, and the close relationships you have with your family, friends, and colleagues at work.

But there is a possible way of life where your gratitude spills over into every part of your existence. I call it a "grateful heart." I almost called this book by the name, *Living Life with a Grateful Heart*. To feel truly grateful for everything and everyone, you need intention, and a daily practice of expressing gratitude, which I talk about at the end of this chapter.

So far, you have read the chapters on listening, vulnerability, humility, forgiveness, regrets, and relationships. When you work on these areas of your life, you are establishing the building blocks that you need to give gratitude the space to grow and float to the top and become a bigger, more purposeful part of your life.

My story

There was the Christmas tree in all its glory. It looked 100 feet tall and with the lights and tinsel, and it sparkled in a magical way. But that's not what really caught my eye. It was the bright red fire engine with its lights flashing and the ladder fully extended up to the middle of the tree that drew me in. Was that for me, or my brother? Or, even worse, did we have to share it?

That was probably 60 years ago, and that memory is still ingrained into my mind. That fire engine kept me fascinated for days and days. My brother and I created a world of our own imagination and used it to entertain ourselves in such magical ways. But like with many new toys, after a while, the magic begins to fade and we are off looking for the next new bright and shiny toy to get our attention.

My parents did all they could to balance the joy they got from buying gifts for us with the lessons of being grateful. The fire engine was probably one of 10–15 presents under the tree, and with so many new toys, it's hard to stay focused on just one. The adrenaline and excitement of tearing open each new present takes over and, before you know it, we are now faced with deciding which one to use first.

When I think back on my childhood, I feel that my parents taught me to live a grateful life. They made sure that I said thank you to anyone who provided service to me, that I was always pleasant, and that I did not take anything for granted.

I think, overall, most people are grateful for many things. A warm meal, a hot shower, a special friendship, a loving parent, a son or daughter, and more. But we can find ourselves adrift when most of our gratitude is focused on physical stuff and things. A new car, a new outfit, a new house, or even a new piece of exercise equipment for your home gym. Many times, these feelings of gratitude go away as hedonic adaptation sets in.

Hedonic adaptation is also referred to as the "hedonic treadmill." Positive psychologists and others who study happiness state that people tend to return to a set level of happiness even after new stimuli increase their levels of happiness.

Using my Christmas story above, as each new gift was opened, my level of happiness increased exponentially. By the time I was done, I was more excited than I had been before I walked down the stairs that morning. But that excitement was short lived as I slowly returned to the same level of happiness prior to opening the presents. This is not a bad thing in my mind, but it can lead us into a belief that the only way to be happy is to constantly buy new things. At some point, we need to be happy with what we have and find other ways to achieve new levels of happiness.

I believe this has a lot to do with being grateful. As I think back on all my years working and having increased levels of financial power, I was able to buy bigger and better houses, join country clubs, and buy newer and more expensive cars. At times, especially as I got older, I found that I was beginning to take some of those new purchases for granted. It was more of a feeling of entitlement than happiness.

Today, as I look back, I begin to look deeper into this idea of being grateful for my childhood, for all that my parents did to provide for me, for all the success that I had during my career. And every day I find new ways to feel grateful and to express my gratitude to others. The more I can express my gratitude to others, the more I begin to feel grateful for everything in my life and those around me.

What do others have to say?

Here are some important questions with actual responses from other men like you:

What does being grateful mean to you, and how do you express gratitude to others?

"Being grateful to me means appreciating what you have in your life. Not simply for material things (which while important might be the least important), but for family, health, freedom, a free society. In terms of how we express gratitude to others, we can do it by being there for them, as a resource for emotional support, advice, guidance."

Anonymous

"To your point, I think most of us live in a world of taking whatever we have for granted, until, perhaps, things take a turn for the worse. I experienced Vietnam, which made me grateful to stay alive. I never forgot that experience and am grateful to this day."

Greg C.

"Expressing gratitude is not that complicated. Tell them. Hug them. I am a note writer, having grown up in a household of letter and note writers. I still do it to this day. When I write a note of thanks, I try to let the recipient know how their action impacted me. Make it personal, relatable."

James W.

What about your upbringing are you most grateful for?

"I am grateful for the example of my parents, and for the values they lived by and modeled for me. I am grateful that they stood by me and respected my choices even if they did not agree with me or understand why I was doing it. The most vivid example of this is when I turned 18 during the Vietnam War. I registered for the draft as I was required to do. I also decided I would apply for conscientious objector status. I am sure my parents—especially my dad—did not understand or agree with this. Yet, my dad went with me to the session of the Presbyterian Church we were members of and supported me as I asked for their support."

Paul A.

"Growing up, I am grateful that my parents always made me feel loved. They emphasized that I was smart and could do whatever I wanted in life, but I had to work hard to get it. My mother's encouragement came about through negative means, my father's through positive ways. Together I got good doses of both. I think they both realized, before I did, that I would have some challenges to address (like being gay in small town Mississippi). They knew about issues that often derail some parents, but they made me confident I could manage those issues."

Anonymous

"I am most grateful for the challenge of growing up without a father, and for the effort that Mum put into 'raising me right' in spite of her fears and grief. Between them, they have given me the power to live as I live today and spend my life helping others."

Stew D.

**As we go through life, there can be a tendency to always want more. A bigger house, a fancier car, expensive clothes, and more. And as we increase our earning capacity, this becomes easier. Take a minute and reflect on all aspects of your life as they exist now. Do you feel grateful for everything?
If so, why, or why not?**

"I'm grateful for a wonderful mother, wife, and extended family. I'm grateful for the better and stronger friendships I have in the area. I'm grateful to have a wonderful home that brings both me and my wife, as well as our families, a lot of enjoyment. I'm extremely fortunate, but I'm also not naive, as I feel I've worked extremely hard. Particularly after having made a few financial mistakes in my 30s and 40s. I'm grateful life got a little easier in my 50s. I've missed holiday dinners and several special events, and passed on vacations to earn what I needed to achieve the things I've achieved."

James D.

"Interestingly, I feel more grateful as I write this than before I sat down to write. Of course, this confirms your point that being grateful is being mindful of your blessings, and for me that means overcoming the corrosive effects of loss aversion, and applying relativity and goal setting. I do suffer the 'wanting more' syndrome and my wife has really helped me not let that get out of hand, to keep me grounded, to remember that having a lot was not the key to my happy childhood. But it's a constant battle."

Ken F.

"Good question. I'm not sure I'm really that grateful for the things we do have, but I seem to have taken my foot off the gas for those 'fancy things' you mentioned, at least a bit. I'm not sure why I don't have that grateful feeling. It may be that life is so hectic and routine that I don't take the time for gratitude. Not sure, but it should be something I examine more closely."

Anonymous

Any other thoughts on gratitude?

"One of the questions I have asked myself and others is how to best balance gratitude with ambition. At some level, they are at odds with each other, yet I believe they can coexist. I would love to have more conversations with growth thinkers on this question."

Brent K.

"A diagnosis of muscular dystrophy has challenged me at times. But because of this I have experienced so many acts of kindness from family, friends, neighbors, and strangers that I am regularly overwhelmed with gratitude."

Anonymous

Your Turn:

If you want the best results possible from this book, answer the journaling questions before moving onto the next section.

What does being grateful mean to you, and how do you express gratitude to others?

_____
_____
_____
_____
_____

What about your upbringing are you most grateful for?

_____
_____
_____
_____
_____

As we go through life, there can be a tendency to always want more. A bigger house, a fancier car, expensive clothes, and more. And as we increase our earning capacity, this becomes easier. Take a minute and reflect on all aspects of your life as they exist now. Do you feel grateful for everything? If so, why, or why not?

_____
_____
_____
_____
_____

Any other thoughts on gratitude?

_____
_____

My challenge to you

Now that you have given this topic some thought, here is my challenge to you:

We have many gifts and people in our lives, and it's important to make sure we know what and who they are. It's also important to make sure we live each day in a way that allows for some time to think and be thankful.

For the past eight years I have risen early and, after my 30 minutes of exercise, I meditate for 10 minutes, then sit with my coffee and journal. It's in this daily quiet time, when I am alone in my thoughts, that I take time to be grateful. Here is a simple daily exercise you can also use:

Get a notebook or journal and write the date at the top of a fresh page.

1. Write three things and/or people you are grateful for, and why. My first one every day is my wife, Jody. I always write something about her that is special to me. This has deepened my love for her and made our marriage bulletproof. You can write about friends, family, your health, your success, the sunrise or sunset, and so on. I think you get the idea.

2. Write three things you are looking forward to on this day. Lunch with a friend, golf with your buddies, alone time reading, date night, or visiting a sick friend. Whatever comes to mind as you think about the day ahead.

3. Write a self-affirmation about yourself. "I am a good husband, I am a wonderful writer, I am an aspiring chef, I am a successful entrepreneur." This is not about bragging but rather recognizing something about yourself that you are proud of. It's a moment of self-love and admiration not intended to inflate your ego, but to inspire gratitude for who you are.

These three simple exercises will, over time, increase your ability to be grateful for even the smallest things in your life, and open your heart to more love and kindness towards yourself and others.

CHAPTER 15

EGO

As I think of ego, I compare it to a two-sided coin. One side is a self-confident and resilient young man who is grounded in his values and ambitions. He understands his place in society and understands that he stands on the backs of others to achieve his success. He walks into a room and people tend to move in his direction. He has a firm handshake, looks you in the eye, and gives you the sense he appreciates you as a friend, colleague, or business associate. He is grateful for your meaningful relationship.

The flip side of the coin is a person who is overconfident, and insensitive to those around him. This is the person who, when you walk into a room, you tend to walk the other way from. You can tolerate him but not for very long. He is the one that will ask for help, but use what you give him for his own self-promotion and growth. His overconfidence and arrogance is distasteful and overbearing.

Learning to develop a balanced ego isn't just taming your arrogance.

It's more about recognizing the fine line between self-respect and self-obsession. It's a balancing act that is needed in order to achieve personal growth and maintain meaningful relationships. The ego is a complex part of who we are and understanding it can make all the difference in the world. When you unlock this knowledge and learn to balance your ego, you can pave the way for a life enriched with authenticity and purpose.

My story

In the first third of my life, up until the end of college, I don't think I thought too much about ego, and can't really recall where my ego was at that time. I was a poor student, with low self-confidence and low self-esteem. When I left school and began my career in our family insurance agency, I found a path that worked for me. My confidence grew as I built my skills in sales and built a successful business with my brother, Chuck. My dad was confident but not a bragger. He was a good role model for me in that regard. Chuck was even more so and helped me to find a balance between success and staying grounded and true to my core values.

I clearly remember at the age of 28, I was given the opportunity to make a presentation to a large multinational manufacturer that was currently with one of the large national insurance brokers in New York City. I was introduced to the CEO by a friend of my father. We had a meeting and he said it would be okay for me to meet with his CFO and make a pitch for the business. I have never worked harder on anything in my life. I spent countless hours at my kitchen table researching the countries they had locations in and trying to learn about local admitted insurance in Mexico and Puerto Rico. I tore apart their current insurance program, reading every single page of their insurance policies. I studied their financials to find misalignment with limits on their policies. In the end, I put together a compelling presentation that they would have a hard time saying no to. From day one, the CFO made it very clear I did not have a chance of getting his business and I had this burning feeling he might be right. But I never gave up.

So, when the call came in from the CFO that I got the business, I was overwhelmed with joy, gratitude, and excitement. I ran into my dad's office to tell him. I was bouncing off the walls. It was our largest account in the office, and I did all the work. My confidence was at an all-time high, my self-esteem was off the charts, and I must say I was acting a bit cocky and maybe even arrogant. Once I settled down, and sat across from my dad to get his reaction, he said two things to me. First, he told me he was proud of me. Hard work does pay off.

Then he said, "Don't let this go to your head." He continued, "Think about all the other people in this office who helped you, including me, and the person who introduced you to the CEO. The underwriters at the insurance companies that helped you find a better solution. There were a lot of people helping you with this win. It's important to always recognize that!"

This was a lesson on what a healthy ego looks and feels like that I am grateful for. This moment in my career was 45 years ago and I easily could have let that sales success go to my head and become a cocky, self-centered person with an unhealthy ego. I have to admit I was feeling a bit like that until my father sat me down and had the conversation about all the other people that helped me.

What do others have to say?

Here are some important questions with actual responses from other men like you:

How is your current ego (healthy or unhealthy) serving you in your life? Now that you're thinking about this, do you feel you need to make changes?

"I think most people feel they have a healthy ego that serves them well in life. But that's a bit of an oxymoron since, for the most part, the level and state of one's ego is something gauged by others. I'd like to think that I have a healthy ego. But what I think and what others think or perceive may be vastly different. I suppose I use (or test) my ego in day-to-day exchanges."

Bob R.

"I believe I have a healthy ego, though some remind me that it tends toward strong. I am strong in my opinions, but I try to understand the opinions of others. My husband sometimes reminds me that not everyone wants to do what I want to do in the way I want to do it. That reminder helps me to be more sympathetic towards others' ideas and ways of doing things. Occasionally, he tells me that he doesn't know why I'm asking his opinion, because I will do what I want to do. But he adds that's OK because most of the time, he agrees it works out well. In my case, I think it's good to have someone who I respect to help me keep my ego in check."

Anonymous

"As I am in my first year of retiring from my business, many things are in transition for me. As CEO of my business, having a strong but healthy ego was important. As my wife has been retired for awhile now, it was pointed out to me that there is already a CEO at home and there is no need for a change or for more than one! I believe most of the time my ego is very healthy, but at times I find myself telling new people I meet more boastfully about myself than is healthy and necessary."

Anonymous

Think about situations where your ego has shown up. (Think about your personal life, your work life, and your relationships.) How has your ego helped you? How has your ego gotten in the way of you becoming the person you want to be?

"I think a healthy ego has helped in the sense that it has influenced self-assurance, self-worth, and self-confidence."

Chuck N.

"Ego is a tremendous asset in business, especially in those situations where you are out of your element. Not sure there is much difference between strong self-confidence and ego. In my experience, ego has gotten in the way in my personal life. With age, I have done a much better job understanding it's not always about winning."

Joseph A.

Throughout your life, you've probably encountered people with healthy and unhealthy egos. How do you typically respond when you encounter someone with an unhealthy ego?

"If I can, I run for the hills. People with unhealthy egos are toxic. I've learned over time that it's never worth the aggravation to invest in the relationship. When I can't run for the hills, like in a client situation, I walk on eggshells to minimize the risk of triggering the unhealthy ego to flare up."

Ken F.

"The world is full of people who do things out of control, self-importance, or ego. I don't do well with those people; I usually see right through their bullshit, and I tend to take them on. There are people who are more politically expedient, who see the challenge as a marathon and that it's best to outlast them. I generally take them on—maybe because of my ego?"

James W.

"Good question. I think avoidance. I just try to avoid people like this. I don't want to engage or interact with people like this."

Anonymous

"I honestly have to say when I meet a person with an unhealthy ego, there is rarely a second meeting. If it is a business situation, I try to find a different person to deal with instead of the person with an inflated ego. Conversely, if I see a person who has all the skills and is a wallflower, I try to get them out of their shell as they have much to offer the people around them."

Charles P.

Any other thoughts on ego?

"It occurred to me that you can think of ego as a shield for good and bad. Good, because it can protect you from the setbacks that life throws at you, and bad because it can create a barrier to human relationships, taking worthwhile risks of failure, and learning from others."

Ken F.

"Whether it's ego or just confidence, or knowledge or awareness, I wish I could have had more of the positive elements of these earlier in my career and in life in general. I think my early years were rudderless—I did okay, but didn't think big or act big, and I think a lot of that has to do with the ego."

Anonymous

"Good topic—the ego. As you rightly suggest, the ego is necessary. It is generally tied to the adult capacity to think critically, assess situations, set goals, make sound decisions, and execute on those decisions. To a large extent, the ego makes us more confident and effective in the world. At the same time, the ego is easily deceived. It can become blind to its dependence on others. It can sadly lose its humility. For in fact, any strength or wisdom has come to us from a Greater Source. We stand on the shoulders of our teachers, coaches, mentors, friends, etcetera. On another important point that you articulated, the ego often runs from emotional vulnerability. This too impedes effectiveness. Emotional intelligence demands vulnerability. Emotional intelligence is critical to team-building and long-term effectiveness. The ego must be in service to emotional intelligence."

Carter V.

Your Turn:

If you want the best results possible from this book, answer the journaling questions before moving onto the next section.

How is your current ego (healthy or unhealthy) serving you in your life? Now that you're thinking about this, do you feel you need to make changes?

_____
_____
_____
_____

Think about situations where your ego has shown up. (Think about your personal life, your work life, and your relationships.) How has your ego helped you? How has your ego gotten in the way of you becoming the person you want to be?

_____
_____
_____
_____

Throughout your life, you've probably encountered people with healthy and unhealthy egos. How do you typically respond when you encounter someone with an unhealthy ego?

_____
_____
_____
_____

Any other thoughts on ego?

_____
_____
_____

My challenge to you

Now that you have given this topic some thought, here is my challenge to you:

I think that people do not spend enough time thinking about ego. If you have an inflated view of yourself and your talents, you should be aware of this and find a way to temper it. It might be hard to do this on your own as, many times, you may be blind to how you behave with others.

Having a healthy ego ties closely to being humble. Having a healthy ego is the ability to balance your sense of self-esteem with your arrogance. An unhealthy ego can be characterized by arrogance, defensiveness, and a need to constantly prove yourself.

Grab your journal and start a fresh page for Ego.

Write down and answer these questions:

- ☐ Are you able to acknowledge and accept your strengths and weaknesses?
- ☐ Are you confident in your abilities, but also aware of your limitations?
- ☐ Are you able to take constructive criticism without feeling attacked or getting defensive?
- ☐ Are you able to handle failure and setbacks without feeling like a failure as a person?
- ☐ Are you able to celebrate the success of others without becoming jealous or envious?
- ☐ Are you able to recognize and respect the boundaries of others?
- ☐ Are you able to maintain healthy relationships with others, without feeling inferior or superior to them?
- ☐ What did you learn about yourself from this journaling exercise?

Here are some steps you can take to work further on your ego:

- ☐ Discuss this topic with someone you trust.
- ☐ Solicit feedback on your answers above.
- ☐ Be open to criticism.
- ☐ Really listen with an open heart and don't be defensive.
- ☐ After this, write how you feel and what you can do to change.

CHAPTER 16

COMPASSION AND EMPATHY

Like listening, compassion can be learned, and it's a virtue that can make all the difference in the world to your happiness, your relationships, and your outlook on your life.

I think all of us have a space in our hearts for some level of compassion. This is something you need to think about and explore. How does your current level of compassion or lack of compassion serve you?

Empathy is a cousin of compassion. The big difference is that while empathy allows you to put yourself in another's shoes, compassion requires a level of action. Being empathic is critically important as a life virtue so learn more about that if you like.

Pay attention to this chapter. Compassion and empathy are critical life virtues that can open up much needed emotional intelligence in all of us. When you get to the journaling questions, take your time to reflect on where you are with compassion and empathy. Then take my challenge and learn some ways to improve your ability to provide compassion and empathy to others.

My story

I was about 12 years old and my mom and dad were taking us on a spring break vacation to Eleuthera, an island in the Bahamas. I remember being in the van, driving from the airport to the hotel, and we passed small villages as I was staring out the window. I saw corrugated steel shacks along the roadside, one after another. Women were walking down the street carrying buckets of water, large baskets of fruit, and even suitcases, all perfectly balanced on their heads. There were other women and men standing over open fires cooking food or at sinks doing laundry. I could not stop looking.

I asked my mom some questions about these people and their lives. I was so curious and interested in learning more about how they live. Are they poor? Are they dangerous? Are they happy? Do they need help? My mom did her best to explain to a 12-year-old that this is how many people in the world live and that we should be grateful for all that we have, and yes, we can find ways to help them. My dad chimed in that we should not leave the hotel property and, when some of these people come walking down the beach, make sure you keep your distance.

So I was hit with this dichotomy of feelings from my parents. They were different people with different beliefs on what I was witnessing outside the van window on the way through a typical community like what you can find all over the world. And it left me wondering what—if anything—I could do to help.

Fast forward to 1998, and I am sitting in a circle of 20 people in a remote part of Nicaragua on my first work trip to that country to build two homes for people living on the edge of survival. I was now 41 years old and just spent an hour touring the village of Las Conchitas, a community of about 100 families located in a remote part of that country, and I was brought back to that trip in the van when I was 12.

This time, I was living with them and working side-by-side to build two new homes made from concrete blocks and reinforced with steel, and a raised tile floor to keep the rainwater and animals out. These houses are built to withstand hurricanes and earthquakes, providing a new level of security and housing. I toured many of the existing dirt-floor homes that have been in their families for generations. The families stood by their homes, proud as could be. The floors and surrounding ground, which is dirt, have been recently swept. The beds were made, and their clothes hung from the rafters in plastic grocery bags. All the homes had mirrors so they could look their best when visitors came to visit.

During the orientation, Bonnie Gordon, the local leader in Nicaragua, was telling us some stories about going through life with blinders on. Horses wear blinders to make sure they always look straight ahead and don't get distracted by anything else around them. That works for horses when pulling a wagon or cart, but it does not work for humans who want to learn more about everything around them. Bonnie asked us to spend the next week with our blinders off. Look at everything and everyone. She said, "If you're curious about anything, ask us," and, "If you want to have a conversation with some of the families, we can make sure we get a translator to make that happen."

I did spend that week with my blinders off, and I have had them off ever since. That simple story changed my life in countless ways. Not only did I fall in love with the people of Nicaragua, but I returned more than 20 times, bringing as many people as I could to experience the transformation that takes place when serving others at this level. It was during those trips that I began my journey toward becoming an evolving man. My heart was cracked open, allowing me to become more humble, sympathetic, empathetic, kind, vulnerable, and loving. It was this trip where I practiced and learned compassion at a deep level, and now I encourage others to do the same. Be empathetic to your fellow human beings and also show compassion by offering help.

I am forever grateful to both Bonnie and Jim Gordon for their role in helping me to evolve into who I am today, and I have the wisdom to know I can still do more.

What do others have to say?

Here are some important questions with actual responses from other men like you:

What does empathy and compassion mean to you? Do you feel you are an empathetic person or that you need to work on this skill, or both?

"Empathy to me is about putting yourself in someone else's shoes and head, and understanding what they are going through and having genuine feelings of concern. By nature I am not very empathetic, so it is something I need to constantly work on."

Joseph A.

"Walking a mile in someone else's shoes.' Not simply imagining what someone else is experiencing, but taking the time to gain an understanding. Not your idea of what someone is going through, but their idea, their feelings, which quite possibly are not at all like yours."

Anonymous

"I've even been told that I need to work on empathy. Once, I was told that I lack genuine concern for my fellow man. I think I'm pretty empathetic with people I know and love. With them, I am patient, kind, happy to share with, and even happy to sacrifice for them. I am ambivalent about others. For the most part, I feel like they can do what they like without interference from me; either positively or negatively."

Anonymous

We live in a world filled with 8 billion people, all with different beliefs and struggles. Issues like politics, racial equality, religion, and sex can be very divisive when discussed. Think of a time when you were in a discussion with someone, and you showed empathy for them. What was the topic and how did you show empathy?

"After George Floyd was murdered, I called my African American friends and had what, for me, were very uncomfortable conversations. I realized I had no idea how they were impacted by racism. In fact, because they are all educated, successful men, I assumed that they probably weren't impacted. Those conversations led me to a completely different understanding of what they and their families had gone through and still go through. Especially their sons, who are my sons' ages."

Anonymous

"A good friend was depressed over his business situation. He knew that I have struggled with that over the years and wanted to talk about it. We did. I shared my experience and how I coped. And then I just asked questions, listened to his answers, and asked more questions. I think he felt better from vocalizing to someone what he was feeling and thinking. I simply communicated that I knew how painful it could be, and that there are ways to ease the pain. I didn't try to solve his problem or tell him what to do."

Ken F.

"In order to ensure that all members of my team got some restand recuperation away from combat, I was moving the team around southern Iraq. It was also an opportunity to give each of them a chance to gain deeper experience for future operations. When I informed one of my junior noncommissioned officers that he was heading 'up country,' he started sobbing and shaking with fear. My view was that the place I had chosen to send him was not so dangerous—I'd been there on numerous occasions. I recognized that this would not be the best response so sat with him and listened to his concerns. In time, he came to see the positives and I put him on the next morning's helicopter. My empathy came through talking and listening."

Stew D.

How have others empathized with you in your life? Give an example. How did that make you feel (i.e., frustrated, hurt, hopeful, at ease, etc.)?

"After my first business failed, I had no money, two babies, credit card debt, and a mortgage. I was blessed to have an unbelievable support system which enabled me to start anew and to chart another course for my career and family. Without the empathy and support of others, we are ultimately alone in the universe and, by definition, in opposition to one another. Empathy is what makes us human."

Chuck N.

"One of my earlier and most memorable moments of empathy toward me was when I was at a pivotal moment in my college life, when the education path I was on was faltering. My father showed me one of the greatest forms of empathy by asking me questions and allowing me to seek a new path, and then supporting it financially. He has always been a great source of empathy in my life and I never forget that."

Phillip E.

Any other thoughts on empathy and compassion?

"Maybe empathy is not about 'fixing' someone else, but about standing with them. Holding them up. Holding each other up to face whatever it is we need to face. I would not be who I am or where I am without those people in my life who held me up. I don't need to list them all, but their names regularly push their way into my awareness. When I remember them, I give thanks for who they are."

Paul A.

"I think this is one of the most important characteristics of a great leader."

Vincent B.

Your Turn:

If you want the best results possible from this book, answer the journaling questions before moving onto the next section.

What does empathy and compassion mean to you? Do you feel you are an empathic person or that you need to work on this skill, or both?

_____
_____
_____
_____

How have others empathized with you in your life? Give an example. How did that make you feel (i.e., frustrated, hurt, hopeful, at ease, etc.)?

_____
_____
_____
_____

We live in a world filled with 8 billion people, all with different beliefs and struggles. Issues like politics, racial equality, religion, and sex can be very divisive when discussed. Think of a time when you were in a discussion with someone, and you showed empathy for them. What was the topic and how did you show empathy?

_____
_____
_____
_____

Any other thoughts on empathy and compassion?

_____
_____
_____

My challenge to you

Now that you have given this topic some thought, here is my challenge to you:

I want you to go through a process of self-awareness by reflecting on how your experiences, beliefs, and societal conditioning may influence your understanding of others.

Think back on your childhood and how you were raised. I know that during my formative years, my parents—and especially my grandparents—held some strong prejudices that spilled over into my beliefs. They became my beliefs, and they were hard to change, but I knew that most of the prejudices I held were not acceptable, and I did not want to pass them along to my children.

The next thing to do is to educate yourself. Read some books, watch documentaries, or sit down and meet with someone you respect that you know has a better understanding of empathy than you do and learn from them.

I want you to try and put yourself in other people's shoes. Imagine what it must be like for people who are constant victims of prejudice and punching bags of these long-established prejudices. You can't turn on the TV without hearing about conflicts around the world. They have existed for centuries and they will continue to exist. But we don't have to ride that train anymore, and we should not.

You may be wondering what your personal shift can really do to change anything. The first thing it will do is to bring you some peace. When you can begin to look at every person for who they are and not put energy towards ill feelings, a considerable weight of inbred hate begins to melt away. Empathy is a strength and not a weakness, yet society would tell you that men need to be strong and not show emotions. This is wrong, and your belief in this must change in order for you to evolve.

You can begin small by spending time listening to your core relationships and being empathetic to their situation. And if needed, show compassion by taking some action to help them. Refrain from dismissing what they are struggling with. Instead of judging, ask more questions. Don't be quick to offer solutions; many times people just want to be heard. You will be amazed at how appreciative they will be for an open ear and gentle heart towards what they are going through.

And finally, if you want to expand your empathy and compassion, research the following examples of recent events that have brought significant changes to empathy and the way society perceives and responds to various issues.

- The #MeToo Movement
- George Floyd and Black Lives Matter
- LGBTQ+ Rights and Marriage Equality
- Mental Health Awareness
- The Refugee Crisis

Pick one of these topics, learn as much as you can, and you will be amazed at how much you begin to peel away your inbred prejudices. You may even surprise yourself by becoming involved in the movement.

CHAPTER 17

CURIOSITY AND LEARNING

Curiosity and life-long learning are tools that we can use to continue to build our knowledge base so that we can bring more light to the world. I have developed a better practice of learning, which is serving me well now in my life. My old way of thinking was pretty narrow and I relied on my current knowledge and beliefs to guide my thinking. Today I question almost everything, looking to learn if there is a better way to go through life. With this kind of mindset and skill set, we can learn to rethink our stances and push away stubbornness.

When was the last time you were in a library, a museum, or an art gallery? If you have never been to the Smithsonian in Washington DC, it is a must. You could spend a week slowly walking from one building to another learning about almost anything you can imagine. These institutions are there for us to learn about our past, our future, and our planet, and to push our minds to better understand the world in which we live.

My favorite pastime is to wander around a bookstore. Walking up and down the aisles looking for a cookbook, or a self-help book, or even history books and biographies. You can get lost in thought and, before you know it, an hour has flown by. Making time to read, watch documentaries, and visit museums is critical to our growth as humans.

Taking off our blinders and opening up to new ideas, new ways of doing things, will help us to evolve beyond who we are today.

My story

I was always a curious little boy; almost nosy to a point. I was always asking questions about everything and anything. My parents at times would be frustrated by my onslaught of question after question. Many times, my follow-up question to their most recent answer was "but why, Mom?" Prompting them to dig for yet another answer. They always encouraged me to be curious about learning, to be a good student so that I can go onto college and get a good education.

It was 1968, I was 12 years old, when on a Saturday morning, the front doorbell rang. I raced to answer it and standing there was a well dressed man carrying a huge suitcase. He introduced himself and said he was interested in coming in to show us an Encyclopedia Britannica set. My parents invited him in and the five of us listened to his sales pitch.

There were 24 separate volumes that all weighed a few pounds and were just beautiful. It looked like they were bound in white leather with gold stamping on the outside, with the volume number and alphabet guide as to what was in that volume. As I leafed through a copy, I could smell the fresh scent of paper and ink. The pages were shiny and filled with pictures and text that seemed to describe anything you could imagine. The volume in my hands had a series of clear pages that included color prints of the human body. There were about ten pages, and the top page was a complete picture of a man in his skin. As I flipped the pages over, they revealed a new photo of what was under his skin. As I continued with this flipping of pages, I saw the organs, the muscles, the veins, and ultimately the skeleton. I could not put the book down.

My parents bought the 24 volume set, which arrived a few weeks later. I insisted that the books go in my room as I had space, and I promised my family they could come in any time to "borrow" one at a time. This set of books was today's version of the internet, and I learned so much over the next few years as I leafed through them. Of course, over time, the information became dated and I think my parents ended up donating them as we grew up and did not use them anymore.

But the encyclopedia set helped nurture my curiosity. I became obsessed with understanding how things worked; how ships stay afloat, how the human body functions, and how our country was formed. My greatest curiosity was around how mechanical things worked and I spent the rest of my youth taking things apart to better understand their function. My dad would take me down to the lawn mower shop in Mamaroneck and ask the owner if we could grab some of the older mowers that he was throwing out so I could bring them home and disassemble them. This launched my desire to take things apart and put them back together. I would spend hours in the garage taking the Briggs & Stratton engines apart. And then I would put them back together. This led to me building Revell model kits and Estes rockets.

I brought this level of curiosity into my entire life and career. I spent 38 years being curious about what risks companies faced that I could solve with risk management solutions and insurance coverage. This deep curiosity led me to a unique risk analysis that helped propel the growth of our company and prepare me for what I am doing now.

And even more importantly, as I matured to where I am now, I began to realize that I was not always right.

What do others have to say?

Here are some important questions with actual responses from other men like you:

Are your beliefs and ideas part of your identity? Is there a world in which you embrace the joy of being wrong?

"I think when 'wrong' turns into a learning exercise, I embrace it. Especially if it's an 'ah ha' type wrong/learning experience; or something like 'wow, I didn't know that!'"

Anonymous

"Sometimes during challenging conversations with my wife, I resort to being defensive or needing to explain myself and be heard, especially if it involves getting constructive feedback from her or others. It is in those moments that I try to remind myself to 'just be curious,' try to learn where my blind spots are, allow for the ego to dissolve a bit and let in some light that another person who loves me is trying to shine. It's hard to do this when we live in a stereotypically masculine environment where boys are trained to be right victors and there is a culture of 'if you're not with us, you're against us' mentality. So breaking apart from the truths we hold steadfast goes straight back to the topic of vulnerability. How can we be curious if we're not allowing ourselves to be vulnerable?"

Noah E.

"Unfortunately, for most of my life, my feelings, thoughts, and beliefs have served as the ultimate veto power. If I didn't feel good about something, didn't understand it, or didn't think it would work for me, I vetoed it! But being wrong so many times in my life, I have come to understand that my greatest lessons have always come from my 'wounds.'"

Tim H.

Who's someone you normally have a hard time hearing? What would happen if you sat down with them just to listen and try to understand their views better?

"I've been told on many occasions that I am not the best at listening. My mind gets ahead of my patience to effectively listen. Need to do a much better job of listening to my son."

Joseph A.

"One thing that has helped me a lot is the realization that exchanging views is not a competition to be won. If I can get out of that mindset, I find it's much easier to ask questions rather than make points, and that really promotes learning."

Ken F.

"There were a number of times in my life when someone who I knew cared about me sat me down and either said some things to me or helped me sort through some difficult things which I would have much rather avoided and helped me to see myself and/or the situation better. Those moments are not easy but they are invaluable."

Paul A.

How can we change the cultural narrative about rethinking? Can you imagine a world in which saying "I don't know" is seen as a mark of confident humility instead of ignorance, and "I was wrong is viewed as an act of integrity rather than an admission of incompetence?

"I believe we can change the culture through education. Teachers can help. Clergy can also assist. Everyday life is a thinking experience. But it is how we live our everyday life that shapes how we rethink our destiny. Saying 'I don't know,' is actually, in my opinion, a reply that warrants respect. Humility could be the appropriate feeling. But oftentimes if I say 'I don't know,' if the subject interests me I might look into it further to find out what might have been the answer. I believe saying 'I was wrong' and 'I don't know' are both acts of integrity."

Charles W.

"We human beings are tricky—we succeed as a species because we are able to cooperate in large numbers, but also because we have a competitive nature that when well-directed, brings out the best of us. Within a unit—family unit, business unit, sports unit, religious unit—we can change the cultural narrative about rethinking if the heads of the unit lead by example."

Ken F.

"I think that world does exist, especially in successful organizations both small and large. It also exists in families, where parents lead by example, demonstrating to the kids respect, integrity, intelligence, and compassion. Sounds corny, but change for the better starts at home."

Michael L.

Any other thoughts on curiosity or learning?

"I believe that being a lifelong learner today is more important to me now than ever. I actually look to get multiple viewpoints from conflicting news sites. It is easy today to find those sources that support my way of thinking. It is very humbling whenever I pursue sources that challenge my traditional thinking."

Anonymous

"Curiosity and learning are what people should strive for in their everyday life. You should at any age continue to want to know about different subjects, which can come from reading, interacting with others, social media, and of course your children."

Charles W.

"There's a great lesson I learned on this from a client. I asked him why he had so many different consultants in addition to me. His response was, 'Because I don't know what I don't know and I have to find out before my competition does.'"

Roger S.

Your Turn:

If you want the best results possible from this book, answer the journaling questions before moving onto the next section.

Are your beliefs and ideas part of your identity? Is there a world in which you embrace the joy of being wrong?

_____
_____
_____

Who's someone you normally have a hard time hearing? What would happen if you sat down with them just to listen and try to understand their views better?

_____
_____
_____

How can we change the cultural narrative about rethinking? Can you imagine a world in which saying "I don't know" is seen as a mark of confident humility instead of ignorance, and "I was wrong" is viewed as an act of integrity rather than an admission of incompetence?

_____
_____
_____

Any other thoughts on curiosity and learning?

_____
_____
_____

My challenge to you

Now that you have given this topic some thought, here is my challenge to you:

I think the best place to begin your curiosity journey is with yourself. You have a tremendous history of experiences such as challenges, failures, successes, and more. Spend some time journaling about your life. The biggest thing is remembering your stories and feelings during certain times of your life. Celebrate all of your successes, remember what you learned from your failures. Begin to make a list of your core values, using this book as a guide. Don't be hard on yourself, but rather celebrate who you are, all that you have accomplished, and how far you have come.

The next area to work on is your relationships. Be curious about who your core friends are. They could be family, your spouse/partner, your therapist, your spiritual advisor. Having these friends is critical to your healthy survival as a human. But do you have someone (or a group of people) who you can open up to, be vulnerable with, and share what's on your mind with, without being criticized or judged? Having that in your life is powerful. Without it there is a chance we can suffer in silence.

Be curious about yourself, be curious about your relationships, and be curious about the world around you. Begin to embrace learning as a daily habit. Make it a point to learn a new hobby, a new language, or something to expand your knowledge in an area you are passionate about.

CHAPTER 18

KINDNESS AND GENEROSITY

Kindness can show up in many ways. Kindness began for me because of my parents' encouragement and nurturing as I was a young boy and man. They established the basics like holding doors open for people, pulling chairs out for women at a restaurant, and helping elderly people cross the street. I think you get it; we have all been told the same thing at one time or another.

I found the Boy Scouts of America definition for kindness in the Scout Law. In the handbook, Boy Scouts of America explains kindness with, "Treat others as you want to be treated. Never harm or kill any living thing without good reason." This was another early teaching for me as I was growing up.

"Do unto others as you would have them do unto you,"—often referred to as the golden rule— and other versions of this show up in the Bible as well. This was repeated to me time and time again in church, in Sunday school, and around the dinner table at home. My parents would say that this is a core principle of our family, to make sure we treat each other with respect and kindness; and that goes for neighbors, friends and, our community at large.

I believe generosity is the twin of kindness. They go hand in hand and when you learn to pair them, your life will change. While kindness means being considerate and helpful to others, generosity means giving something such as your time or financial resources. You can't be kind without giving something of yourself, and you can't be generous without being kind.

There are countless opportunities in daily life where you can be kind and generous. Think about that as you go through your day today and tomorrow. Were you kind to everyone you met? Did you tip a little extra for your meal and thank them for great service? Is there an organization you have been thinking about volunteering with or donating to and you just keep putting it off?

My story

So many times growing up, I would go to my mom with people problems I was facing. From being picked on in elementary school, to difficult people I met while trying to grow my business. She always gave the same advice. She would look me in the eye and say "Honey, the best way to deal with people like that is to kill them with kindness." This was repeated to me the entire time she was alive.

She lived her life this way and always made time for everyone. When we would go out to dinner in a restaurant, she always struck up conversations with the wait staff. From the dishwasher (if she could find them) up to the maître d' and the owners. She had a wonderful way about her, going through life being kind and making people feel good about themselves. I don't ever recall a time when her kindness backfired.

I have embraced her motto "kill them with kindness" and use it on everyone as well. I suppose that some people have taken advantage of me because of that, but I believe that I have tipped that scale on this one and always came out on top. And when I say on top, I mean that the people around me felt respected, loved, and appreciated.

As I have aged, I now perform random acts of kindness on a regular basis. The goal here is to give something of yourself to someone at a time when your spirit moves you to do so. This feeling will pop up in all of us, but we tend to push it down. I'm suggesting when you feel this coming on, act on it. You can change the direction of someone's life with the smallest of gifts.

There is a young woman at the local deli where Jody and I pick up food all the time. She is one of the kindest persons I know and always goes the extra mile for us. I was picking up lunch the day after Thanksgiving, and something came over me to give her such a generous tip people would say I was crazy. She refused at first, but I insisted. I saw her again a week later and she pulled me aside with a tear in her eye. "Thank you for the money last week. You don't know much about me, but my daughter will now have the Christmas I wanted to give her because of you. I am grateful to you for that." A random act of kindness that she will remember forever and maybe have a little more faith in herself and the world in which she lives.

What do others have to say?

Here are some important questions with actual responses from other men like you:

How do you define kindness and why do you think it's important?

"Kindness is doing something for others when it is not required or expected. It's making someone's day better when they are not expecting it."

Jeffrey C.

"Kindness is not complicated, it is largely unqualified. Listening, supporting, not judging, being 'in the presence.' As I get older, kindness has become more and more important. Being kind makes me feel more alive. And more a part of the community; the way things were back when we lived in small villages, and everyone helped one another."

James W.

"I think we sometimes use 'be kind' and 'be nice' interchangeably. What I realized this week is they are not the same thing. You can be 'nice' in the moment, but still hate the person you are being nice to. Kindness is something more."

Paul A.

When was the last time you did something kind for someone? What did you do and how did it make you feel?

"Today I held a door open for someone at the post office and this person was quite a ways from the door. I paused for a moment to consider whether I needed to stand there and hold the door and then I thought to myself, I will wait and hold the door. It always makes me feel good."

Phillip E.

"I have a friend who recently lost her husband rather suddenly to pancreatic cancer. She was struggling with some maintenance on her bicycle since her husband used to take care of it. So, I offered to help her by showing her how to perform the maintenance so she could do it in the future. It became a special moment for both of us. She appreciated my time and efforts and I enjoyed being of assistance."

David C.

"A few weeks ago, a kitten in desperately poor health walked up to me in Brooklyn. It was knocking on death's door. I didn't know what to do, and initially felt 'not my problem.' A woman walked up and asked where the cat's mom was. I didn't know of course. She gave me courage to help the kitten, and somehow the way she spoke with me sparked inspiration. Next thing, I'm in a car with the kitten on the way to the vet. Weeks later, we still have the kitten, he's healed from several aggressive infections and diseases, and found his full time home with us. While I recognize my own compassion and kindness in this story, I credit the woman in the street with the initial compassion and kindness—she started it, really. Yes, I was open to receiving it, but she's the one who sparked the compassion and kindness in me. It's a somewhat complicated example of kindness, because it required someone else to make the first move and bring out the best in me."

Noah E.

Who is the kindest person you know? What makes them kind?

"I think my son Tom is very kind—he's a teacher working in a charter school in Philadelphia. His students are mostly minority kids growing up in tough neighborhoods and he cares so intensely about them and their capacity to learn. He wants them to really understand things and to love learning so they can have a better life. He's not only kind and caring to them, but he's the same way with other family members, and friends. I just love being around him."

Anonymous

"My mom, who sounds a lot like your mom, is the kindest person I have ever met. Literally never said an unkind word about anyone, and always went out of her way to help anyone with an issue. Sadly, she passed away when I was in my early 30s."

Anonymous

"The kindest person I know is my wife. She is an excellent cook and on a regular basis will bring her homemade meals to others in need. She fully gives of herself and is available to everyone. What makes her kind is her nature, I don't believe it was necessarily her upbringing, it's just who she is and who she wants to be. I am fortunate to be married to such a kind person."

Charles W.

Any other thoughts on empathy and compassion?

"It's a trait that some people are born with but that for me developed through an understanding of how lucky I have been most of my life."

Joseph A.

"A few weeks ago, a visiting priest from Africa took time after the 11 a.m. Mass I was in to remind the congregation that 'Kindness is understood in all languages.' It does not need to be described and can be seen and understood by all."

Matthew M.

Your Turn:

If you want the best results possible from this book, answer the journaling questions before moving onto the next section.

How do you define kindness and why do you think it's important?

_____
_____
_____
_____
_____

When was the last time you did something kind for someone? What did you do and how did it make you feel?

_____
_____
_____
_____
_____

Who is the kindest person you know? What makes them kind?

_____
_____
_____
_____
_____

Any other thoughts on kindness?

_____
_____
_____
_____

My challenge to you

Now that you have given this topic some thought, here is my challenge to you:

Kindness to yourself

You must first be kind to yourself, and that comes in many forms. I know that I have flaws, imperfections, bad habits, and more. But I spend time forgiving myself, I spend time looking for the goodness inside of me, and I spend time looking for opportunities to work on myself. None of us are perfect and there is always room for improvement. So, working on ourselves to be better husbands, parents, friends, business partners, and human beings is a way to be kind to yourself.

Making good decisions about exercise, mindfulness, nutrition are all ways to be kind to yourself. Instead of looking at these as difficult habits to bring into our lives, we need to see it as a form of kindness and love to ourselves. I'm 66 years old while writing this book. I have lived a full life, but I fully intend to live to 100. And to do so, I need to be kind to myself. My physical wellness vision is "to be physically independent at the age of 90." This vision is what drives all my healthy habits. I live every day to the fullest and make time for exercise, good food choices, moderate-to-no alcohol, and daily meditation.

Whenever I think about skipping my morning workout or meditation, or look at an Oreo cookie, I always ground myself in my vision. This is our time, and we must do all that we can to wake up every day in a positive mindset and feeling healthy and happy. It begins with being kind to yourself. And continue to be kind to yourself when you deviate from your plan. I certainly am not perfect with my self kindness, but my goal is to get it right more than I get it wrong.

Get into the regular habit of doing something fun. Go for a walk, get a weekly massage, have lunch with a friend, go see a movie. Do something that lifts your spirits each day, and treat yourself with something special each week. Tie in some of this as a reward for starting a new healthy habit. I workout three days a week doing body weight exercises. As long as I complete the three days, I treat myself to a massage the following week. It's my own incentive and reward for making the effort. Think of something that works for your lifestyle and interests, and implement it.

Kindness to others

"Kill them with kindness." My mom was right; when you have this mindset, you become more fun to be around, you become more friendly, you become more inspirational. Others feel drawn to you, friends will like you more. Complete strangers will smile back at you, but you must smile first. When you are kind to another human being, something magical happens and you brighten their day. I know this can sound like a big pie in the sky, but trust that being kind to others will make you feel better as well.

There may be people in your life that are caustic, and you have a difficult time being around them. With these people you need to set up boundaries, as being kind all the time may allow them to walk all over you. This is when you might need tough love or to make difficult decisions to limit your time with them. But you can *always* still be kind when you are with them.

Generosity

I do not know your financial credentials. But I understand from my personal experience of traveling nearly 20 times to Nicaragua and the Dominican Republic that 80% of the people on our planet live in what we would describe as poverty. And in the United States, we do not have to look far for people who are living on the brink of survival.

Knowing this can be helpful as we reflect on our own lives. Are there people or populations that could use help from me either in the form of my time or financial help? Sometimes a little help can go a long way to lift up a person and, at the same time, give you a warm feeling in your heart.

Be kind to yourself and others, and be generous with your time, your talents, and your financial resources.

CHAPTER 19

LOVE

This is the last virtue that I will cover in this book. I purposefully put it last because it really is an overriding theme in your life when you learn to practice all of the virtues we just covered. In my mind it is what happens when we begin to evolve and open our hearts to practicing everything we have covered so far. It is not a virtue that can stand on its own. I wanted to call this out in case you find yourself wondering if you can have love without the other virtues.

Love can show up in many different forms. People talk about the love of food, cars, fancy clothes, vacations, cooking, relaxing, and so much more. I actually love to cook, play golf, watch the sunrise, and spend time with friends and family.

But this chapter is about the love of our fellow human beings. And not only giving love but receiving love, which we all need. And before we can love others, it's important to love ourselves—with all our faults and emotions. Self-love and self-care help us be able to love others, to create long lasting relationships.

Love can be complicated, and many men have a difficult time expressing love in words, actions, and emotions. Some of this may be influenced by how you were brought up and the environment that you live in. If you were not nurtured in a loving kind way, it may be hard for you to do this for others.

When I think of love I always begin with my wife, Jody. It is a love that has been nurtured for the 14 years we have been married, and has taken on different forms since we have met. It has evolved and continues to evolve. Today, it can be described as a deep connection that includes physical desire, emotional care, affection, and a deep respect for who she is. She is my greatest love, and where I spend effort on a daily basis to nurture our love for each other.

From there, my love flows out to my children, their partners, my grandchildren, and the rest of my extended family. Those relationships differ; they ebb and flow as to how much effort I put into them. I believe I have a lot of work to do here and I make efforts on occasion, but can always do more. It's one area of my life that I beat myself up over and wish I would make the change. I envy families that have huge annual family reunions. That would be fun for sure.

I spend time loving myself as well. Feeling loved is as important as giving love, so it's important to feed yourself love as well. I have faults, like everyone, but I don't identify myself by those faults, rather as a balanced work in progress. Even at 66, I realize I have work to do in all areas of my life.

When I think of a person who I care for, my heart begins to soften, my worries seem to disappear, and a smile comes to my face. I get an overall feeling of happiness, kindness, and gratitude. When I call them or see them, it always warms my heart. Where is love in your life? Some people can harden over time and have difficulty maintaining love. It can derail when there is poor communication, unresolved conflicts, infidelity and betrayal, or neglect and lack of effort. I cannot imagine a life without giving or receiving love, but I know there are people who live that way.

To me the highest form of love is unconditional love. This is giving love to those in your life without expecting anything in return. Once again, if you can get better at the previous eleven virtues, you will evolve and be able to give unconditional love. This sounds to many as impossible, but believe me when I say it is a peaceful, kind and nurturing way to love. If you give something away, like love, with the expectation that something must come back, or a condition must be met, you will spend a lot of time being disappointed.

Let's all think about how we can find a way to nurture love for ourselves and others as we read this chapter.

My story

My parents were my first example of what love looks like. It formed the building blocks of how I express my love today. I have had to change out some of those blocks because they did not work for me, but overall when I think of my parents' love for each other it was grounded in affection. They cared for each other, they cared for me, and gave me unconditional love. That nurturing at a young age will always be ingrained in my mind.

When my mom died, I received note after note from her friends, and everyone had a story of love and kindness that she shared with them. One note in particular caught my attention as it came by way of email from someone I had forgotten even existed.

For 30+ years we had a housekeeper Lenora who came every week to help my mom clean our house, keep it organized and always ready for family and visitors to sit down and chat about life. She was more of a friend and family member than a housekeeper. When Lenora got cancer and had to go get chemo treatments, it was my mom who drove her and was with Lenora until she passed. Early on, when Lenora would come, she would bring her son, John. He came when school was closed and would wander around our house and backyard. I have faint memories of this young boy but don't recall paying too much attention to him as he was much younger.

When my mother died, I received an email from Lenora's son John and he reintroduced himself. It was 40 years since John was at our home and I was taken aback by the reconnection. He told the story of how my mother had cared so deeply for his mom and how my mother also cared for him, and he felt like he had another mother. He shared the story about how when he was headed off to college, my mom was the one who drove him there. When they arrived there was a problem with his outstanding balance on his tuition. He was devastated as he had no money and thought his parents had made the payment. After some discussion, my mom made the $5,000 payment right there on the spot so that he could stay and go to college. He promised to pay back every penny to her and, in fact, he did pay her back, and he became an entrepreneur who built a large tech company in Boston. He credits my moms kindness, generosity, and unconditional love as the reason for his success as an entrepreneur, father, and husband.

I was so surprised at what my mom had done and that she never told anyone. This email from John and his story was another jolt of energy to increase my capacity to love unconditionally.

What do others have to say?

Here are some important questions with actual responses from other men like you:

What does love mean to you?

"To me, love is the ultimate expression of how we value others. If we place no value on someone, if we don't care whether they are healthy and happy or whether they suffer, we show no love for them. The way we love, the depth and ferocity of our love, in the end shows how we value, how we care about, another."

Chuck N.

"Love means transparency, a willingness to be open to those whom we love. A willingness to take on the most fierce conversations that we so don't want to have."

Phillip E.

Thinking back to your childhood, how did your parents love you?

"I was very fortunate to have parents that were very supportive, very loving, and caring. My mom knew how to express it openly—she was the one who would say, 'I love you, you are my kid,' things like that. My dad was not as verbal about it, but his actions certainly showed it; lots of golf together, attending as many games of mine that he could, backing me up when I needed it. It was a demonstrated, but not verbalized show of love. My dad was also a disciplinarian, and would say things like, 'I'm doing this because it's the right thing to do, and it will help you.'"

James W.

"Not very much at all. Even before Dad's death, my memories are of love being a function not a feeling. Very little outward expression. After Dad's death, Mum became more distant as she dealt with her grief—that continues to this day with my sister and I and my children. No spontaneity for fear of showing vulnerability."

Stew D.

"Growing up, I knew I was loved. I felt it. I don't know how else to describe it. Sometimes I questioned my parents' love for me, but in the end, I never doubted it. Their love for each other was harder to see or feel. They lived apart as much as together. I would say they couldn't live with each other and they couldn't live without each other. Ours was not a 'touchy, feely' family. As a child, I don't recall ever hearing anyone in my family say, 'I love you' to another family member. But I know I felt it. Even now, when my brother signs a note to me with, 'Love,' I get a strange feeling. Even more so when he says it. But we are trying to be more demonstrative. Not sure why. My brother says others need to see and hear us express love more often, and it's good for us to say it."

Anonymous

Still thinking back to your childhood, how did your parents express love to each other?

"Their expression of love between each other 'matured' over time, but that 'through sickness and health until death do us part' thing rang true throughout their lives and through my dad's Alzheimer's disease. Having never driven, and with no extra money for taxi fares, my mother took a bus from Hawthorne to White Plains, and then a second bus from White Plains to the County Home at Grasslands (Westchester Medical Center) twice a week to see her husband who couldn't remember having breakfast. That's love."

Bob R.

"Big time sacrifice—time, money, and maybe even their individual happiness. They held hands at the dinner table (yuck!), they locked themselves in their bedroom when Dad got home from work to debrief on the day and prepare themselves for the hectic evening ahead with six kids running around, and they never ever kept secrets."

Ken F.

Any other thoughts on love?

"I think it would be nice to love others the way they want to be loved. I wonder if I would even know how to find out how others wish to be loved. Perhaps it's part of the communication function; just ask?"

Phillip E.

"I usually end a lot of messages to my buddies with LUM, 'Love you man.' I find that, many times men typically only communicate love to another male friend when it is standing over a casket, when we could have said it when it really could have mattered. I try to always let them know how I value their friendship while we're still alive!"

Anonymous

Your Turn:

If you want the best results possible from this book, answer the journaling questions before moving onto the next section.

What does love mean to you?

_____

Thinking back to your childhood, how did your parents love you?

_____

Still thinking back to your childhood, how did your parents express love to each other?

_____

Any other thoughts on love?

_____

My challenge to you

Now that you have given this topic some thought, here is my challenge to you:

I put the chapter on Love this far into the book, because I believe you need to understand everything I have written about up until now, in order to truly give and receive love.

Learning how to express love is critical to enhanced relationships. I believe it is so much more than just saying the words "I love You."

You can be kind, generous, have compassion, be forgiving, and so much more and yet true unconditional love can be hard to attain. But it is possible.

I want you to get out your journal and go back over what you have written on each of the previous chapters. Use a highlighter and highlight one thing that resonates with you from each chapter's journal questions. Write them down again as a summary for yourself. Use this exercise to refresh yourself on what you have learned so far.

The next thing to do is make sure you love yourself. If you struggle with that, don't be afraid to get some help. Therapy can do wonders to help you reframe who you are and help you know that you are enough. I also think daily journaling is helpful. Beginning each day with writing a self affirmation has become my daily ritual. It looks like this:

I am a good _____.

Fill in the blank with anything that moves you. A good father, a good husband, a generous giver, an inspirational writer. Try and come up with new affirmations every day and also repeat those that are core to who you are. A good exercise is to begin with writing 25 of these all at once. Keep writing until you come up with 25. Reread those every day for a month. This is a good way to kick start this process.

Over time, as you begin to love yourself more, and then lean into loving others, your heart will open and come more alive as a part of your being. All the other virtues get a chance to play in your heart as well. Gratitude, kindness, generosity, listening, and forgiveness are all part of a loving heart.

SECTION 3
A DEEPER DIVE

SECTION 3

INTRODUCTION

These 12 virtues that you just worked on are foundational to living a better life, being a better human, and giving you a stronger foundation for your journey ahead. This is a journey to last your lifetime, so take it slowly but also take it seriously. Most of these virtues have everything to do with relationships; your relationship with yourself and with others.

I pulled these next six chapters out of the life virtues because I believe that these are very personal and can't be handled in the general, broad-sweeping ways that the life virtues can be. These next few chapters are really about *you*—your individual life and how you can truly work from the inside out and create a vision for how you will live the rest of your life.

These are no less important, but I felt I should separate them. I start with self-care which is all about taking care of yourself. This covers both physical and mental wellness and is critical to having the energy you need and the capacity to work on the life virtues in Section Two.

CHAPTER 20

SELF-CARE

As a young man, self-care looked to me like an annual physical, a semi-annual visit to the dentist, trying to limit my hangovers to the weekend, and eating whenever I felt hungry. During my 38-year career, I was on the road a lot, so fast food was my friend. Stopping at the deli on the way into work for a bacon and egg sandwich. Lunch at fast food (McDonalds, KFC, or another deli sandwich) because I was always in a hurry to get to my next appointment. It never crossed my mind that this food that I was ingesting was slowly eating away at my insides and creating havoc that later reared its head.

As far as exercise, I did very little. Sure, I was one of those that joined the gym every January because the gym offered a good membership deal. And I went for a while, but never did much because I had no idea what to do. Then when I could afford a trainer and a really nice gym, things got a little better. When I had a scheduled appointment, I felt an obligation to show up. But if I didn't feel like working out, I would just text him and cancel. In reality, while I did learn more about working out and I always enjoyed feeling sore the next day, it was sporadic at best.

Jody and I spent a year in semi-retirement as we phased out of our careers. And it was during that time that our health took a nosedive. We entered this phase of life with the attitude that we deserve to live the retirement we dreamed of: travel the globe, eat and drink to our hearts' content, sleep late, watch a lot of television, and live life to its fullest. The problem was that this "retirement" experiment led to weight-gain, daily hangovers (I started drinking heavily again), always feeling tired, and always searching for more. We quickly realized that it was not sustainable.

That's when self-care for us really began and we have made this a priority in our lives. I cannot undo all the damage I have done. But on the other hand, with proper nutrition, sleep, exercise, emotional health, and natural supplements, we can reverse the trajectory of health and bad habits and behaviors. This in turn will help us live longer and better. We have a health care team that, besides our normal battery of doctors, also includes a nutritionist, naturopathic doctor, physical fitness coach, and more. We are always looking for and researching the latest information to help with this journey.

My story

Dr. Cohn looked at me perplexed. He had been my General Practitioner (GP) for 15 years and could not understand the results he was looking at. "Your cholesterol is off the charts and your blood sugar is high as well! I don't understand it, you're only 45, you're in good shape. You don't smoke, you exercise, you don't drink in excess. I guess it may be hereditary." Sure, both my parents had high cholesterol and blood pressure, so I chalked it up to being in my genes. But I still did not like the fact I was being prescribed meds for these chronic illnesses.

What I did not share with my doctor was the stress I had in my life at the time which probably exasperated the problem. My marriage was failing, I was drinking too much, I wasn't really working out like I should, and I had picked up the habit of smoking cigars. On top of that, my diet was filled with fast food restaurants and poor eating choices.

Turning 50 was a pivotal point for me. My mom had dementia, my dad was a functioning alcoholic, and my health continued to get worse. My stress was getting worse. Poor sleep, unhealthy habits, and anxiety became the new normal for me.

At first, I just accepted it. But as I spoke to others, researched online, and read some books, I learned there was a better way. My first stop was a visit with Dr. Gibson in Ridgefield, Connecticut—a naturopathic doctor who helped me look at my body and my health in a different way. After extensive blood tests, a generous supply of natural supplements, and advice on nutrition and healthy habits, under her guidance, my life took a turn that I am forever grateful for.

She was the one that convinced me that meditation would dramatically change my mental wellness and, after her preaching that for three years, I finally made the leap. If you had asked me the day before I started if I would ever meditate, the answer would have been no. Today I can say with all the confidence I can muster, everyone should meditate!

Once Jody and I moved to Connecticut from New York, we found a new local naturopath doctor. I continued on my journey with Dr. Dana Krete's sound advice and counsel. I also found a new GP who believed in the work of Dr. Krete, so I have created an integrated team of physicians who care for me.

If I knew what I know now when I was 25, I would have changed the course of my habits and routines. I have no regrets, but depending how old you are, you do not need to end up shortening your life or creating ailments because of poor lifestyle habits.

I have a good friend who does not get annual physicals and whose mantra is "why look for trouble?" That is one option, but I would suggest that it's not the one you should take. Self-care is important for so many reasons. We get this one life; we should treat it like it's our only one. It's funny how we might take care of our car better than we take care of ourselves.

My self-care program touches on physical and mental wellness. It's more of a ritual now and it has enhanced my life beyond words.

What do others have to say?

Here are some important questions with actual responses from other men like you:

Do you have a self-care program in place and, if so, what does it include?

"Yes, my focus for self-care is based around three key areas: energy, strength, and mobility. While I do lack consistency between my own faults, and having five kids at home, I do strength training four to five times per week, create an evening and morning routine to focus on enough sleep, and do some form of morning and evening stretching/mobility work. I drink a lot of water, and a daily green drink, but struggle with food choices at times. I intermittently fast every weekday between 12–18 hours."

Brent K.

"My self-care program is eating super-healthy, regular exercise, both cardio and weight training, and the consumption of vitamins and supplements I take daily. That said, it has been a journey to reach this 'more than semi-regular' routine. I have indeed put family time above my time, and continue to do so as it makes me happy. Yet, as I get older I have still managed to create just enough 'me time' to work on my health."

Roger L.

"My 'plan' is more physical than emotional, and more moderate than yours. Moderate exercise, moderate alcohol, moderate diet restraint. All things in moderation."

Anderson B.

"All I can say is I try to get a good night's sleep, exercise with some frequency (not frequently enough), and eat healthily. But there's nothing programmatic about any of it."

David D.

**Putting yourself first comes hard to many.
If you are the type of person that puts yourself last
when it comes to care, are you willing to change?**

"I've neglected getting a therapist for a long time, partially because I'm stubborn and partially because I don't always want to do the internal work. Truly though, I'm dishonoring myself, and those around me, when I make an active choice not to work toward improving myself. Yes, I'm willing to change, but it's taken a long time of being stuck in my ways before arriving at this point where I'm taking action. I recently started seeing a therapist on a weekly basis, for the past six weeks. Leading into each session, I feel resistance bubble up inside me, and I wonder how I'll be able to fill the hour of time. By the end of the session, I am stunned by how much there was to discuss, and have a renewed sense of excitement, wonder and patience for myself and for those around me."

Noah E.

"I wouldn't say I put myself last, but definitely not first. I am more than willing to change, particularly recognizing that as we age it is so critical to do self-care. After all, if we don't take care of ourselves, we aren't going to be of any use taking care of others."

Bill M.

Any other thoughts on self-care?

"Something I've learned through coaching my clients is the relationship between self-care and self-love. I find that people who struggle with self-love, also tend to struggle with self-care. When someone is low on self-love (e.g. perhaps they're extremely critical and judgmental of the way they look), it's difficult to find the motivation to put themselves first and stick to healthy self-care habits. Healthy self-care habits form more easily when someone loves themselves enough to make their own wellness a priority."

Christopher R.

"I actually consider self-care more about making sure you avoid things/people/activities that make you unhappy. We all tend to say yes when we really mean no. I have really focused on saying yes to only those things that I truly enjoy. While not always possible, it does wonders on your ability to enjoy life."

Steven S.

"After 40+ years of practicing law, 37 years of marriage, and raising 4 children and getting them in and through college, business school, and now medical school, I've gotten into a routine of prioritizing the needs of those around me over my own. That's a tough paradigm to break."

David D.

Your Turn:

If you want the best results possible from this book, answer the journaling questions before moving onto the next section.

Do you have a self-care program in place and, if so, what does it include?

_____
_____
_____
_____

Putting yourself first comes hard to many. If you are the type of person that puts yourself last when it comes to care, are you willing to change?

_____
_____
_____
_____

Any other thoughts on self-care?

_____
_____
_____
_____

My challenge to you

Now that you have given this topic some thought, here is my challenge to you:

Putting yourself first is easy for some people, and that's great. But what does that look like for you? Just like my mom, I am a people pleaser and much of my energy has always been to help others, to make sure everyone around me has everything they need, and not pay too much attention to how I feel. That was okay in my 20s and 30s, but not as I passed into my 40s. Over time, especially now that I am in retirement, I am focusing more on myself. So when I look back, I wonder what I would feel like if I had implemented everything I do now back when I was 25.

I cannot change the past, but I can change today and every day moving forward, and you can too. Take this idea of self-care seriously. Schedule in exercise, learn how to meditate, begin writing in a journal each morning. Make sure all your doctor visits are up to date. This is such a critical part of being a human being. Let your medical team have full access to you so they can uncover something that might need attention.

I have outlined below some steps you can take to begin to build a vision and plan to change your self-care program. And self-care should include physical and mental wellness.

Action items:

- **Get all your medical visits up to date.** This is the most logical starting point, especially if you are behind. This is your one shot at taking care of your body. Begin this selfcare journey with a good assessment of your health.
- **Practice good oral hygiene and get to the dentist.** This sounds like an obvious thing to do, but there are plenty of people who do not get annual checkups or cleanings. Ignoring your oral hygiene now can create havoc as you age so pay attention to this.
- **Schedule in exercise. Join a gym or get equipment for home.** This might be the number one area that can change how long you live as well as the quality of your life as you age. Even walking 20 minutes a day can add on years of healthy living to your life—and this costs you nothing! Find a local gym and get an assessment. You will be surprised that you can also build a community there, which further helps your mental health.

- ☐ **Start tracking your sleep and get into a sleep routine.** I believe that a good routine of exercise supplemented by a good night's sleep will do wonders for your health. Try getting between seven and eight hours of sleep a night. Get into a routine of going to bed at the same time and waking up at the same time. And think about a pre-sleep routine. No food or alcohol two hours before bed. No TV an hour before bed, and definitely do not watch TV in bed. Watch TV in a chair or couch and reserve your bed for sleeping. Think about a warm shower before going to bed and reading a part of a book to help settle you down for a good night's sleep. And no other electronics an hour before bedtime. If you really want to give yourself a chance for good sleep, leave your phone in another room.

- ☐ **Read part of a book every day.** I was never a good reader until I began my career; then I became a self-help book junkie. Today, I still love a good self-help book but also have begun reading books about historical people and events. Reading daily can improve brain connectivity, reduce stress, help with sleep readiness (better than TV!), lower blood pressure, and so much more. Learning about anything and everything can be an important part of your life. Try visiting your local library and touring the shelves. You might be surprised by what you see there. Another one of my favorite things to do is wander around a bookstore. Grab a book and sit and read.

- ☐ **Learn how to meditate.** I began meditating in 2015 and it changed my life. I am such a different person now because of my meditation practice, I can't even remember living life without it. It was also the hardest thing I have ever tried to begin, as I have always had an active mind and had trouble sitting quietly. There are so many places where you can find meditation support. There are apps you can download to your phone and also many online meditation videos. Try starting with guided meditation, that is what I did and it was very helpful.

- ☐ **Nutrition and alcohol** Eating right and drinking in moderation are good basic ways to feed your body. Spending some time with a nutritionist is a good way to start. Weaning off of what I call my "comfort food" has been hard. But I take baby steps every day and step away from sugar, red meat, and processed food. I have learned to enjoy cooking so I have better control over what I put in my mouth that way. As far as alcohol goes, it's a daily battle for me. The bottom line for me is that even one drink will give me a hangover and the feeling of a foggy head for an entire day. This is a personal choice for all of us, but if you feel that you are drinking too much and it is affecting your health and relationships then you should look at this carefully.

- **Journaling** I hope by now you are getting used to journaling and it becomes part of your daily life. Try first thing in the morning or at the end of the day. Some self reflection is always helpful to clear your mind and calm you down. It also allows for you to dream and imagine a better life for yourself. Always make sure to celebrate any successes and make a note of it in your journal.

I hope this has been helpful and gives you a path to focus on self care.

CHAPTER 21

SEX AND INTIMACY

If you are standing in a bookstore and leafing through this book to see if it's for you, and this is the first chapter you flip to, it's not that kind of book. This chapter is not filled with top three sexual positions to reach orgasm or even ways to entice your partner to want to have more sex with you. But it is about a way to bring intimacy into your relationship that could in turn improve your sex life and also improve your emotional connection, affection, and your overall well being with your partner.

When most people think of sex, they think of the physical act of sex that includes desire, arousal and the physical pleasure and sensations that come with intercourse and orgasm. And having great sex can be a huge lift physically and emotionally, but bringing intimacy into your sex life is important because it brings you closer in a deeper, more intimate way. Being able to be vulnerable and ask and share what feels good will enhance your sexual experience and bring you closer.

You and your partner need to be able to share your desires, fears, and emotions so that you feel connected on a deeper level. This takes trust, communication, and a mutual respect for each other. And if this is not part of your sexual relationship right now, there is work you can do to get there.

I am not a relationship expert or a sex therapist, but I am in a relationship with Jody that allows us to talk about all of this in a safe, kind and loving way. It's not always easy, but we have given each other permission to open this dialogue up when we feel we need to.

Sex is an important part of my life and always has been, and maybe it's important for you too. Being intimate and having an orgasm feels amazing. When I was 18 and having sex for the first time, it was always about the orgasm. Almost 50 years later, not so much. And this is where it gets personal because most men really don't share this part of their lives with anyone else. Some guys like to brag, and many of them are crude when they do brag. But how many men really sit down with their buddies and talk about issues like low sexual desire or erectile dysfunction?

Many men will complain that their wife or partner doesn't want sex any more, or that it's not the same. The truth is that we change. Our bodies change, our desire changes, our ability to have an erection can change. And erectile dysfunction (ED) for men can shut you down completely from having sex. You should not be embarrassed about this, nor should you ignore it. Go see your doctor and discuss it with them and your partner. Putting this topic on the table will take vulnerability for sure.

I would also like to note, getting addicted to porn can change how you look at sex and can always leave you unfulfilled when you and your partner don't have sex like what you see when watching porn. If you struggle with pornography, this is also not something to ignore.

If you are uncomfortable talking about sex and intimacy with your partner, then speak to your doctor or even a therapist. You should not be ashamed to make this a part of your growth as a man. If the desire is there, but you're having difficulty performing, then take some time to work on making some changes. I will go deeper into some steps you can take in the challenge section of this chapter.

My story

My family had a vacation home in New Paltz, New York. For 30 years, from the age of 8, I learned many skills there that helped form who I am today. Construction, hunting, firewood management, skiing, hiking, spelunking, drinking alcohol, and sex. Most of this was taught by my dad.

I was about 15 when my dad felt it would be a good time to talk to me about the birds and the bees. My younger brother, Chuck, and I were sitting at the kitchen farmhouse table across from the franklin stove with a roaring fire in it. It was late, and I was about to go to bed. My dad was on his fourth or fifth scotch, and I'm sure I had a few beers under my belt. Yes, drinking was a part of our family life. I think my dad was nervous and waited till he got the courage to give us the birds and the bees chat.

The conversation was awkward, to say the least. My dad's tongue was loose from the alcohol, and his words were crude, visual, and barbaric. He described, in detail, how to get things started and finished, using his hands as puppets on what to do to your sex partner. Like how to get her in the mood and warmed up, for example. He may have mentioned condoms, but I'm not sure. I do not recall if he ever included the word "intimacy" in this verbal instruction manual. What I do remember though is etched into my brain. I love my dad for all he was, and I forgive him for his transgressions. He did the best he could with what he had.

The first thing I did after writing this part of my book was to call one of my sons to ask about *my* chat with *him* on the birds and bees. Thankfully, he said I mentioned condoms, and safe sex. He recalls we were both uncomfortable. I felt a relief that I did not carry forward what my dad taught me in such graphic detail.

When I was a teenager growing up, most of my friends were having sex way before me. They would brag about it, sharing all the details as proud young men and making me feel inadequate and unsure when and how my sexual journey would ever begin. I was a late bloomer for sure, and it was a rough start on so many fronts.

But as I think back on my sexual journey, from the back seat of my 68 Plymouth Barracuda and my college dorm room, to procreating children, I notice now how everything has changed for me. My second marriage to Jody began with intimacy, not sex, and that has made all the difference in the world for our relationship. We communicate openly about this subject and encourage others to do the same.

I was never taught how to bring intimacy into sex or into my relationship. I have it now, but wished I was taught earlier. There are no regrets, but I believe that, as men, we must be able to bring intimacy into our relationships, especially with our partners. The sex part can always change and grow, and you can experiment and communicate what feels good to you and your partner. And all of that becomes easier when there is intimacy.

Intimacy is all about the close ties you have with certain people. It can grow over time as you begin to care about each other in a deeper way and become more and more comfortable with that person. It can include physical and emotional closeness, and even a mix of the two, such as sex. But sex does not always have to be about the orgasm.

What do others have to say?

Here are some important questions with actual responses from other men like you:

What does intimacy mean to you regarding your spouse or significant other? And how has that changed over the years?

"It's interesting that you combined the words. I have always thought that the physical activity of sex was just that. Intimacy was about love and care. Sometimes they go together, even simultaneously, but not always. It's fun to be intimate without sex, especially as I have aged. Intimacy just became much more enjoyable. Physical changes to my body make sex less important. That doesn't mean I don't still enjoy it."

Anonymous

"It's various little things; a brush of a shoulder, a hug, a certain look from across the room, sex itself. And how has that changed over the years? When you factor in one kid, it decreases. Then with the second kid it decreased even more."

Rino P.

"Like many men, I suppose, I thought of intimacy and sex in terms of my selfish masculine needs. I was not interested in foreplay—and certainly not conversation—before, during, or after sex. It was always a self-centered act on my part. One of the most intimate skills I had to develop was listening. Giving someone your complete interest and attention is one of the most intimate things you can do. I think my wife came to cherish that more than anything."

Tim H.

What were you taught about sex as you grew up? How has that changed over the years?

"My dad sat me down with a book from the library, and in pretty much every conversation, I would imagine there was an adequate level of awkwardness. The sex part was more of a learning experience with me and my wife learning and growing together, which has helped to create the bond. We have relationship books that have questions that we have gone through to learn more about each other and what the other needs/wants, and that has been nice."

Vincent B.

"I never had the experience of my parents talking about the birds and the bees. Growing up in a strict Catholic family, that was not going to happen. It was not uncommon in my day to be a virgin when you got married, thus the learning process would just begin. Frankly, that experience made the process much more exciting and adventurous."

William M.

"My mother and father both talked about it openly. Dad was a doctor and always feared I would knock someone up, as he saw it in his practice all the time. I got the sex and underage drinking conversation from him when I was in 9th grade."

Charles P.

"All my sex education came from the science class at school. The rest came from fumbling around and learning through trial and error. Being married to a midwife, we have very open discussions about sex, and we were both a part and remain a part of our children's education. They still come to us (they are now 23 and 25 years old) to ask for advice."

Stew D.

What changes would you like to make about the intimacy and sex that you are currently having? What changes would you like your partner to make?

"The lack of physical connection, sex, and intimacy makes it difficult to really connect overall with my spouse. I mean, of course I love my wife, but I also miss having fun and having a sexual relationship. Since this is sort of recent, I haven't figured out how to 'fix' it and it's very frustrating for me. I don't see a fix or solution."

Anonymous

"Intimacy with my wife grows for me when we do stuff together; I think it grows for her when we talk. And I know she wishes we talked more. I can't tell you why that is hard for me—it seems to take huge amounts of energy. Not because of her, just because. And we humans are all about conserving energy to be able to survive. So it's hard for me."

Ken F.

"I am very satisfied with our current sex life. It was always good but over time has even improved which is counterintuitive."

Robert W.

Any other thoughts on sex and intimacy?

"I have taught myself to suppress my sexual desires at this point in my life. Perhaps looking at sex through the lens of intimacy is a path back to enjoying both with my spouse? I also have issues with fear of rejection; which oftentimes prevents me from furthering this conversation for growth in this area. It's easier to suppress than to ask for what I want."

Phillip E.

"It can be the best connection, and the worst thing about a marriage when it's not working well. It spills into the entire relationship."

James W.

Your Turn:

If you want the best results possible from this book, answer the journaling questions before moving onto the next section.

What does intimacy mean to you regarding your spouse or significant other? And how has that changed over the years?

_____
_____
_____
_____

What were you taught about sex as you grew up? How has that changed over the years?

_____
_____
_____
_____

What changes would you like to make about the intimacy and sex that you are currently having? What changes would you like your partner to make?

_____
_____
_____
_____

Any other thoughts on sex and intimacy?

_____
_____
_____

My challenge to you

Now that you have given this topic some thought, here is my challenge to you:

I have friends who are open with me and say that they are living in a sexless marriage. If both partners are okay with that, then maybe not much needs to change. But if one of you still has the desire but the other has just shut down, then there is work to do. If you are in a solo relationship and dating, then most of the comments below will apply as well.

Here are some common reasons couples can lack intimacy in their sex lives:

- Lack of communication. Sex and intimacy is not an easy topic to talk about for many couples. But without open communication, nothing will change.
- Stress and anxiety. These are regular side effects of life, but they can hamper sexual activity.
- Relationship issues. Maybe you have unresolved conflicts, a lack of emotional connection, or trust issues. These can all contribute to a poor sexual relationship.
- Body image concerns. Our bodies change, which can lead to self-esteem issues and can affect our confidence in the bedroom.
- Mismatched libidos. When you both have different levels of sexual desire, this can create challenges.
- Performance anxiety. This can be a big issue, especially if it's related to erectile dysfunction.
- Lack of novelty or variety. If your sex life is predictable and routine one of you may become bored.
- You or your partner are lacking self-care. Cleanliness, healthy lifestyle habits, emotional wellbeing all play a role in a healthy and active sex life.

There are more reasons couples move away from an active sex life and also an intimate sex life. If you are struggling, then perhaps talking to a counselor, therapist, or your healthcare provider is a good place to start. There is no lack of resources available to help you start your journey towards a healthier and more intimate relationship that includes better sex, if that is your goal.

But the very first place to start is to have a conversation with your partner. If you currently don't talk about sex, then this may be difficult. But you should start somewhere. Maybe just let your partner know that this is something you want to talk about and set up a time that works for both of you. Giving a little warning will give both of you time to prepare. And if there is too much tension, back off and try again.

Here are some suggestions:

- Agree on an appropriate place and time. Privacy with no interruptions is key.
- Always use "I" statements. A therapist told me once that it is always better to begin a conversation like this with "I" statements to express how you feel. It's not about blaming the other person. "When you say or do (say the behavior, ex. "pull away from sex with me") it makes me feel (explain your emotion, "ex. "unloved")." Instead, try "I feel (explain the emotion) when…" without adding blame.
- Express your desires and needs. This can be hard, but share your desires, fantasies, and needs in an open and honest way. Ask them to do the same. If they are uncomfortable, then give them a pass. You are not going to get this done in one quick meeting.
- Listen like you have never listened before. And you don't always have to respond. And definitely don't react to what was said. Don't raise your voice or blame them for what is happening. Respond in a loving kind way.
- Agree on some next steps. And thank them from a kind and loving place in your heart for having this conversation. The goal here is to move the conversation forward.

Sometimes it's also a good exercise to grab a clean page in your journal and write some stories about when you first met. Where you were, what you were doing, how you felt when you saw each other for the first time. Write about any of the special moments in your life that brought you closer. Think of this as a highlight reel of everything that's happened that involved happy and memorable times. Share some of this with your partner. Ask them to do the same exercise.

When you bring back these memories of when you first fell in love, when you had sex for the first time, the wonderful times you have had, it reminds you of why you fell in love in the first place. Yes, life gets busy, we get distracted, and maybe our interest in our partner wains. But it doesn't have to be that way. Invest in these exercises, get some professional help if you need it. But above all, work on your relationships to bring back some of the passion, sex, and intimacy that was once there.

CHAPTER 22

MARRIAGE

I am not a marriage expert. But I have been married twice and have 40 years of experience in married relationships. The purpose of this chapter is to get you thinking differently about this sacred union. Even if you're divorced, single, or married, there is something we all can learn about the container and process of marriage.

Let's look at the process of marriage. We meet someone, fall in love, ask the big question, then have a ceremony in front of witnesses where we make verbal and written commitments. Maybe we celebrate with family and friends and grab some time for a honeymoon. We arrive back home and probably head back to work. Then we spend the rest of our lives with our partner, maybe creating a family as well.

Now let's look at what I call the container of marriage. This box of sorts that we live in once married, bound by a contract, commitments, rules, and emotions. We coexist inside this container that is fully enclosed and that at times can feel small and limiting. Marriage has been referred to as a ball and chain where we also need to live happily ever after.

I think we can rewrite all of this. Marriage for me is different today. Jody and I met later in life. We were both in marriages that were not bringing us what we needed at that time, and were in the process of completing that season of our lives. We both had evolved as humans, personally and professionally. There was so much we had in common and, at the same time, we each brought different things to this new relationship.

When we decided to get married, we decided it would be different this time. Since we are both big learners, we began our relationship with lots of research on what makes a good marriage. We read books, saw a marriage counselor, looked at other successful marriages, and made a lifelong pledge of being committed to each other and always finding ways to deepen our relationship.

Marriage takes compromise, humility, empathy, vulnerability, sacrifices, and deep listening. We all have to be aware of our emotions and know when we need to step away from a conversation or put it on pause for the sake of not escalating into an argument.

Relationships are hard. They take effort, intention, flexibility, negotiation, compromise and so much more. Marriages are even harder because you are always together. And in this phase of life for Jody and me, we also run several businesses together as partners. So our time together is wrapped up in many different ways.

In the challenge section at the end of this chapter I give us all some things to think about and some ways to bring us closer to our partner.

My story

Or, rather, my parents' story. My parents were my guides on what a marriage should look like. My dad was a hard charging marine, an entrepreneur, a volunteer, a home handyman, and a loving husband. Since he was building a business and wanted to provide for us, he was up early and out of the house before I woke up for school. We got to see him at night for dinner and on weekends.

My mom was a stay-at-home mom. My dad always made reference to that and how important it was to have a mother be able to stay at home to care for us kids. And of course, as I think back, I loved that I had a mom who was always there for me.

As a couple, they were pretty amazing. I could tell they were in love as they were always expressing love to each other in the form of laughter, serving each other, providing gifts, holding hands as they walked, and saying nice things to each other. Words of affirmation were always being tossed around, and there was lots of gratitude to each other.

They did fun romantic things too. They danced the Charleston at weddings, they shared friends, and my dad often left love notes for my mom in front of the coffee pot.

They communicated well. Most communication was done in person. Maybe they had a quick call during the day sometimes for things like, "what time will you be home for dinner?", or "can you stop at the store on the way home from work and pick up some milk?" My parents would catch up during our family dinner. Who they saw, what they did, and what the plans might be for the weekend.

But there was also a dark side. When I think back to my earliest days, I remember them fighting a lot as well, usually at night after we had gone to bed. Not all the time, but enough that I can remember one specific instance that is clear as day. It was late and the loud screaming woke me out of a deep sleep.

As I lay there listening, I could not make out the words, but it was loud. Then I heard their bedroom door open and out they spilled into the hallway. Now I could hear them better. But I was afraid to get out of bed. I just lay there hoping it would stop. Then, I heard my sister come out of her room and start crying and asking them to stop.

My brother opened his door and did the same. As I got out of bed and found myself staring and listening to the scene unfolding, I was scared; worried that someone was going to get hurt. My mom was laying there in the hallway yelling at my dad. My dad was trying to coax her back into their room and encouraged us to go back to bed. He was not yelling, but he was forceful with his statements.

The next morning and day, not a word was spoken about the incident. Chuck, Susan, and I spoke about it, but that fight was not the first time or last time. It was part of their marriage. Love, kindness, and fighting and yelling. That was the basis for my early learning of marriage.

Over time, the fighting stopped, or maybe once I moved out I was not exposed to it. But as they aged, I was able to see how much they cared for and supported each other. They lived interesting lives. My dad had a property in New Paltz, New York, about 80 miles from their home in Mamaroneck, New York, where he would spend Monday through Friday then come home on the weekends. My mom had dozens of friends and filled her life with all of them and her nine grandchildren.

In the winter, they would head to Stuart, Florida, from early January through early June. When my mom's dementia set in, their lives became complicated. They still showed care for each other but it was hard on my dad to watch my mom continue to get worse. Eventually they moved into a memory care facility, with my mom getting the care she needed and my dad living down the hall in an apartment.

My dad's excessive use of alcohol eventually killed him, leaving my mom alone for her last year. It was sad to see how they lived, but it seemed to work for them. I have modeled my marriage differently. Jody and I work hard every day to stay connected in all the right ways by practicing all the virtues in this book. There is a deep love and respect for each other, and the ability to grow individually and as a couple.

I love the process of marriage that Jody and I are in and the container that Jody and I have built together. The walls never feel like they are closing in. In fact, I feel like the box is getting larger every day as we grow and bring love, kindness, listening, and more into our relationship.

No matter what state your marriage is in, remember that at one point you met, fell in love, and decided to spend the rest of your lives together. Read what some of the other men say about their marriage, and then work on yours with the challenge at the end of the chapter. And, of course, don't be ashamed if you need professional help. Do all that you can to create something that is everlasting.

What do others have to say?

Here are some important questions with actual responses from other men like you:

What were the reasons you got married in the first place, and do those reasons still exist today?

"We got married 36 years ago because we really 'fell' for each other. We were really in love, and loved spending time together. Unfortunately, those reasons don't exist today. We really don't have a lot in common and we see life from very different perspectives. I think we're together because it's easier than not being together."

Anonymous

"I got married because I loved my girlfriend at the time and wanted to share our lives together. I wanted to grow old together, have a family, and share my life with her. She is incredible and challenges me to be the best version of myself. It was 17 years ago this December. And yes, in fact, the reasons we got married are actually stronger today. We have challenging times—more so these days with the kids—but we do it together and are united. We still say that our relationship with each other is the most important one we have. Our love, our bond, and our desire to have a shared vision for our future is what holds us together."

Vincent B.

How is being married making you a better person, and how does it provide happiness?

"Marriage is hard work to make it endure over time. I work at listening, being a little softer with my feedback, appreciating her perspective, and celebrating her accomplishments. All of these efforts certainly make me a better person."

James W.

"The patience, love and vulnerability we both bring to each of the roles deepens our relationship every day. It gives us certainty in the relationship and in ourselves. It makes us feel that we truly belong to something important and through this, our generosity to each other and the people we serve grows."

Stew D.

"Being married has made me a better person in many ways. My wife is an immigrant, as I am. She was born in Sicily and then her family moved to Belgium. Italians in general are very giving, joyful, festive, people. Family events are true festivals. My wife is an excellent homemaker, mother and spouse. Her willingness to give of herself and share has shown me a side of life I never knew."

Charles W.

What are some of the aspects of marriage you struggle with?

"We have different love languages. Sometimes that causes resentment. I have mellowed quite a bit because I see all the things she is and focus less on what she is not."

Anonymous

"Managing life goals is likely my largest. We share some goals, but not many hobbies. I like to camp, ski, and impulse travel. She can't ski, will hike but not camp, and likes to plan trips in advance. Our kids make travel seem more like a chore than fun for her, so we don't travel often."

Rino P.

"The only two areas where we sometimes struggle are first, in our relationship to money. We deal with this by sitting down weekly for the business and monthly for the family accounts and work through the challenges. The second is a different sex drive. We seem to hit a happy medium, then not, but we talk about each of our needs and support each other."

Stew D.

Any other thoughts on marriage?

"My decision to get divorced was the toughest in my life but was also the best decision in my life. In my relationship with my new partner, I often reflect on my behavior from while I was married to ensure I avoid making the same mistakes again. Especially understanding my personality better, and letting things go that are not really important. Also, trying to better listen to my partner's point of view and understand what is driving it."

Joseph A.

"Over the years, I have witnessed many great examples of what defines a strong and healthy marriage. Also unfortunately a few too many that weren't. I'm blessed to be in a strong, healthy one. My wish is that everyone can experience happiness and be happy whether it is their first or second or third, etcetera. Being able to share your life with someone you love is a blessing."

Anonymous

"The grass is always greener on the other side. I have many things to be thankful for, especially when I see a friend's marriage collapse. All relationships require a certain level of work and, with all the little things to do in life, it does require work to plan for your most important relationship."

Rino P.

Your Turn:

If you want the best results possible from this book, answer the journaling questions before moving onto the next section.

What were the reasons you got married in the first place, and do those reasons still exist today?

_____
_____
_____
_____
_____

How is being married making you a better person, and how does it provide happiness?

_____
_____
_____
_____
_____

What are some of the aspects of marriage you struggle with?

_____
_____
_____
_____
_____

Any other thoughts on marriage?

_____
_____
_____
_____

My challenge to you

Now that you have given this topic some thought, here is my challenge to you:

I think we could all agree that we know someone who is either divorced or in a marriage that, for all intents and purposes, has run its course. Or the marriage is in critical condition and needs some intervention and drastic measures to revive it. If this is you, you are not alone and I want to give you hope.

I find myself sometimes wondering about the process of my marriage to Jody. In particular the early stages of love, curiosity, exploration, and growth that were such fun and happy times. Fast forward to today and, at times, I think back and wonder why the spark and passion may have diminished. When I find myself thinking this way, I always try to reframe my thinking. The passion and spark is there, we just need to work a little hard to see it. That might mean practicing many of the virtues in this book to constantly keep us close and also keep the fire alive. We are always doing what we can to bring in as much fun, exploration, excitement, and joy to our relationship to keep the spark alive.

Those early stages were exciting times, and it's the process we went through to fall in love. And all of those experiences and memories are the building blocks and foundations of a marriage. That is what led us here in the first place, and those memories should never fade. Finding a way to be grateful that we met lasted this long is something to celebrate.

If your marriage is healthy and you're nurturing each other and getting what you need from each other, then congratulations! You should celebrate your union and make sure you continue down this wonderful path. Always share and celebrate with your partner. Acknowledge how much joy they bring to your life.

But even as you celebrate, know all relationships can use help so that they continue to grow and evolve. And if you are in a relationship that is on life support, please try getting some professional help. Sometimes getting a third party to intervene with conversation and therapy will do wonders to bring you back together, if that is what you want.

It's amazing how humans change over time. Our desires, our passion for fun, sex, holding hands, or long walks together, are all things that, at one time, may have been at the core of your relationship, and maybe now they are missing.

Repairing your relationship or taking it to the next level begins with communication. You must be able to explore your feelings, your desires, and your ability to provide what your partner needs in order to work on your relationship.

As I said at the beginning of this chapter, I am not an expert on marriage, nor am I a certified therapist or marriage counselor. And if you need that kind of help, please search it out. But for now let's try this:

1. Grab your journal and start a new section entitled "Falling in Love." Start writing about when you first met your partner. When, where, and why you fell in love. Go back in time and write about your emotions during the first few years of your relationship. The first kiss, the first time you said "I love you," the first time you had sex. All of these should be positive memories and bring a smile to your face.

2. Next, begin to write about all that you have accomplished together over the length of your relationship. Your careers, your homes, your vacations, and your children if you have them. The idea here is to go back in time and write about the building blocks of your marriage and relationship.

3. Make a list of everything about your partner you are grateful for. Even the smallest things like how they giggle at your silly jokes, or how well they cook. Keep writing, and when you have a long list, go back and read it. Keep coming back to this list and adding more.

By now you should be feeling pretty good about your partner and your life together. And you also may be feeling like there could be more. Things have changed and you want to bring back some excitement into your relationship.

So the next step will be to start a conversation with your partner. Let them know what you are working on and that you want to begin a process of looking at how you can work together on your relationship to make it better. This may not be easy, especially if this is not something you normally have done in the past. So this will take kindness, vulnerability, forgiveness, humility, and amazing listening skills. Everything you have learned in this book! Plus a little patience.

Maybe agree to set aside some time to talk when it works for both of you. Maybe ask them to do the same exercises you just did above. Then, when you meet, you start by sharing what you wrote. This may be hard at first and if you get stuck, take a break and come back to it. Maybe it becomes a weekly meeting you have over your morning coffee.

Ask them a lot of questions.

- What do you need from me to make your life better?
- What is one bad habit I have that if I stopped it would help our relationship?
- What is one thing about me that you love the most?

Hopefully this goes well and you can answer the same questions for them.

Then, dream a little and make some plans.

- Let's start date night. We take turns planning it each week.
- Let's go to the movies.
- Let's start exercising together.
- Let's start a sport or hobby together.
- Let's plan a weekend away.
- Let's think about our retirement; where will we live, what will we do?
- Let's throw a dinner party for our closest friends.

Jody and I begin almost every day with our coffee time. We catch up on the kids, our jobs, our friends and our relationship. We ask ourselves the questions above and always spend time dreaming together about our future. We agree not to let things sit and stew for too long. We are open and honest about our needs, our desires, and our feelings. We agree that our relationship can always be better, and we are always working on it.

It's not always easy and there are times that we struggle. But we always go back to our core reasons and memories of why we fell in love in the first place. Living with the same person inside this container can be hard. But it is also a container that can be overflowing with all that makes you both feel happy and loved.

CHAPTER 23

GRIEF

I have had my fair share of grief, as I am sure you have as well. And the longer we live, the more grief will show up on our doorstep. It is not something we can hide from so we need to find ways to process this grief so that we can continue on with our lives.

It seems like my life has been on a roller coaster of losing family and friends. My dad died of alcoholism and a year later my mom died from Alzheimer's disease. My ex-father-in-law and my current mother-in-law both died from stage four pancreatic cancer. My brother, Chuck, died in October of 2022 after a long battle with ALS. And most recently we lost our 12-year-old dog Max. All of these deaths have hit me in different ways and I carry the memories of everyone, including Max, in my heart and soul.

Grieving the loss of a loved one is an incredibly difficult and deeply personal experience. People will tell you time heals all wounds, including grief. Even though it may be true, it is not always easy to hear from others, especially early on in the process.

Some typical emotions that show up when grieving are shock, denial, anger, guilt, depression, sadness, and finally, for some, acceptance. No matter what you are feeling right now, you are still here and the person you lost would want you to keep living your life.

If you are grieving right now for the loss of a loved one, then embrace it. If you are in pain and sorrow then you are feeling what you should be feeling. But as you read more of this chapter and the challenge at the end, imagine a world in which this sorrow is not a burden, but that the memories of your loved one lives on inside of you and you feel their presence. And if the pain is so severe that it is affecting your own ability to cope, then get some professional help. Don't ever be afraid to get help when you need it.

My story

It was Friday July 10, 2015.

I was sitting on her bedside, holding her left hand. My son Christopher was sitting on her right side holding her right hand. Her breathing was shallow and short, her chest barely moving up and down, but it was enough to see she was still alive.

Having read all the pamphlets that were provided by hospice, and the recent update from the nurses, we knew she was at the end of her 82-year life. Looking at her peaceful face and labored breathing brought an ease over me. Her eight year battle with Alzheimer's was about to end. Christopher had tears in his eyes as we heard my mom take her last breath and then a loud, longer exhale.

It was almost instantly that she felt cold and lifeless in my hand. I put my ear to her mouth to see if she was still breathing just to confirm what I knew. I kissed her on her cheek and forehead then looked at her peaceful face. "Christopher, I think she is gone." As I said those words, I looked back at her and something magical happened. I felt a calmness come over me and, as I continued to watch, a shape like her body rose and came out from under the sheets and up through her chest and went straight up. To this day I believe it was her soul leaving her body. It validated my belief that we are here in body and spirit, and when our body wears out, our spirit continues to live in some form.

We called the nurses, and they did some preliminary checks and then called the doctor to do the official confirmation of death. We all sat in silence for a while before the coroner came to get her body. Soon, my brother and sister came and we all began the celebration of her life.

I called my two other sons and some family members to share the news. Then some of her best friends. The conversation was always positive, kind, loving, and sincere about what a wonderful person my mom, Ann Rollins, was. My dad died about a year earlier and, in my mind, she was on her way to join him.

At the time of her passing, Christopher and I were playing in a three day golf tournament at Siwanoy Country Club in Bronxville, New York and we had two more days of playing. How could we possibly stay focused with what we just witnessed?

The next morning, standing on the par five fifth hole, I looked at Christopher and recanted on how I just made par on the last four holes. "You are playing great dad, stay in the game," he responded. It was at that moment that I heard my mom say to my dad, "Hey look, Markie is playing golf with Christopher, let's watch them for a while."

I envisioned them having morning coffee just like they did every day for decades. I played the best round of golf I ever had and attribute it to having my parents both watching and commenting. I chatted with them a bit and started to realize that they were living inside of me and seeing what I could see with my eyes.

To this day, I believe that everything good about me came from them. All my best qualities and habits came from them. My mindset, kindness, courage, love, humility, and forgiveness came from them. I do not miss them because they are always with me. They guide me, support me, encourage me, and help me when I need it. This is how I handle death. This is how I celebrate loved ones. This is how I can continue to live my best life ever, with their continued guidance and love.

I read recently that when someone you love very deeply dies, part of their soul ends up inside of you and they continue to see the world through your eyes. With this belief, I know they see what I see and help me make the right decisions.

It's what drives me to be kind, thoughtful, spiritual, grateful, and forgiving. Forgiving of my sins and theirs. We are not perfect, but we can strive to be the best we can be to ourselves and to others while we are alive.

As you read the journal responses for this chapter, think of your own stories of grief from losing a loved one. Spending time in your journal writing about your story, your feelings, and the process you went through or are going through is a great exercise. Make sure these loved ones live in your memories and that you share your stories with others.

What do others have to say?

Here are some important questions with actual responses from other men like you:

Thinking of a loved one you have lost, can you describe your grieving process?

"Shock, anger, sorrow, each one present at different times. The shock passes first. Acceptance follows, then emptiness; a void. The void lasts years. Pain. It gets better. There's still a 'hole.' I'm thinking of my parents' passing. Mom died at 57, after a seven-year bout with metastatic breast cancer; the last two years being particularly brutal. And my dad died at 61, fourteen months after my mom. He got sick at 40 with Hodgkin's lymphoma. He was one of the earliest to get treated effectively, but the treatments took a toll."

Anonymous

"My father passed away recently, on January 9th, 2022. He was 94 years old and lived a wonderful life. He contracted COVID-19 in the Fall of 2021, which compounded some health issues he was dealing with. So, his passing was not unanticipated, but the feelings of grief were new to me. His passing was not easy for my sister, mother, or me. My grieving process was centered around his military diary. I discovered it after going through some of his things upon his passing. My mother knew of his diary, but had never read it. I started reading it on my flight home and could not put it down. It revealed a time in my dad's life before I was born and before he was married to my mom. I took it upon myself to dive deep into his military experience and ultimately created a historical journal of his entire life to share with my family. I spent about a month preparing the journal which, in itself, was cathartic for me. My only regret was not having the opportunity to read his diary prior to his passing so that I could ask him some questions."

David C.

How did your life change because of losing that loved one?

"I'm not sure I know how to answer this question. I do regret that I didn't make more time for my father when I became an adult. I was always chasing success and keeping busy. I do make time for my sons and always will. I guess I learned that lesson the hard way in regretting not making more time for my dad."

Anonymous

"I lost both my parents. Mom at 78 from cancer and Dad at 91. I also have lost three close friends Jim (63), Brandon (48), and Doug (67). These losses have moved my wife and I always say to each other, 'Now's the time. We can plan to be healthy and active until we are 75, more if we are lucky, less if we aren't.' I like to say that I've gone from saying 'no' for 40 years when I was working and raising a family, to saying 'yes' now. Losing someone whose life was cut short just underlines that mantra."

Ken F.

"It's an inward reflection. By looking at how they lived, I look at my own life and how I am not living it fully. It adds an increasing sense of urgency to not delay life's goals."

Rino P.

How do you honor or celebrate that person going forward?

"How I honor my dad: Having never graduated high school himself, yet having an appreciation for higher education, I arranged for two scholarships to the Pierce Partners Scholarship Program at Franklin Pierce University. One in my name, and one in my father's. And although he said, 'if you can't afford it, you shouldn't have it,' for individuals who have the dream to attend college (some being the first in their family), money shouldn't keep them from being able to do so."

James D.

"By living and appreciating everyday. By embracing the good with the bad, having belief in myself, belief in the goodness of my fellow man, and optimism for the future."

Michael L.

"I always think of my mom and her goodness. I think a lot of people would use that word to describe her. I try to be more like that, especially with our family."

Anonymous

Any other thoughts on grieving or death?

"A life cut short is far more difficult to deal with, and a death where there is no closure is unimaginable for me (why I have made a habit of saying 'I love you' to those I love)."

Chuck N.

"I have learned that grieving is an unstructured process that oftentimes does not have a finite ending. Memories of the past can resurface, bringing back feelings and thoughts. Grieving is different for everyone. It may take longer for some people. For me, I have many fond memories of my father which make me smile when they come to light. There are a few sad times in between as well."

David C.

"Grieving is so hard. You have a hole in your heart when you lose someone. Remember all the wonderful times together you had. Memories are so important. They keep your loved ones in your soul. I agree that we all grieve differently. No one should tell you how, or how long, to grieve. It's all personal."

Ronald R.

Your Turn:

If you want the best results possible from this book, answer the journaling questions before moving onto the next section.

Thinking of a loved one you have lost, can you describe your grieving process?

_____
_____
_____
_____
_____

How did your life change because of losing that loved one?

_____
_____
_____
_____
_____

How did you honor or celebrate that person going forward?

_____
_____
_____
_____
_____

Any other thoughts on grieving or death?

_____
_____
_____
_____

My challenge to you

Now that you have given this topic some thought, here is my challenge to you:

As I said when I began this chapter, there is no right or wrong way to grieve. But I think it is important to grieve in some form and fashion. The key is to acknowledge and accept your emotions. Do not bury them. And if you have buried them, maybe now is the time to work on that.

No one really knows what happens to us once we die. There are theories, there are stories of people who have died then been revived and live to tell a story of what they saw. But all we do know is that the person we loved is not here in their physical form. Or, at least in the form we were accustomed to.

My challenge to you on this topic is pretty straightforward. I want you to pick one person who has died, leaving you feeling a tremendous loss. It could be a mom, dad, sibling, child, or close friend. Find a quiet place, and maybe make a cup of coffee or your favorite tea or drink. Grab your journal and open it to a new page. Grab your favorite pen and begin writing a letter to them.

This letter must be written from the heart and not the brain. What I mean by that is, don't try hard to think of the right words, just begin to remember them as they were. Their smile, some of the funny things they said to you, what it was about them that always made you happy. I want you to be in a good place, feeling warm and happy. Almost as if they were sitting right across from you.

Write this letter in a way that you are trying to make them feel that you are safe, happy, and continuing to live your life the best way you can even though you miss them so much. Here is a framework for the letter that might be helpful:

Dear. . .

As I sit here in deep thought, I can see your smiling face.
(Talk more about what you see.)

Having you here in my thoughts reminds me of the time. . .
(Write a meaningful story, or several stories, that you carry around with you.)

I want to thank you for a few things.
(Write about everything they did for you, things they helped you with, how they changed who you are as a person, i.e., I am such a better person because of the way you. . .)

While I miss you so much, I feel you with me many times.
(Make a list of when you think of them and how it makes you feel, i.e., when I first get up I always think of you and it brings a smile to my face, when I am struggling I think of our fun times together to bring me back to a happy place.)

And now I want to tell you about my wonderful life.
(Write as much as you want, but always be positive. Write this as if you are able to see them again for the first time since they passed and you're excited to share how good your life is.)

I want to tell you about some struggles in my life as well.
(We all have difficult times in our life. Bring some of this in if you feel it would be helpful to you and if in your heart you want to share it.)

End with some kind, thoughtful words.
(Remind them again how they impacted who you are today.)

I want you to do this with a pen in your journal. Make mistakes, cross things out, write a few versions, work on it for an hour at a time. It might take a few weeks, but I believe it will be a healing process and begin to reframe your loss. In the end, if you like, create a typed version and share it with others that you think would enjoy reading it to help them grieve and honor this person with you.

On the next page is the letter I wrote to my brother, Chuck, after he passed away from ALS in October of 2022.

A Letter to My Brother after He Passed

Charles J. Rollins

August 22, 1959–October 19, 2022

My Dear Brother Chuck,

I am grateful for so much.

Growing up, you were always willing to go outside the rules a bit to have a better experience or greater fun. We led each other into trouble but always managed to come out safe.

We grew and learned together in Boy Scouts, spending time at New Paltz with our family, riding our Honda 50 dirt bikes, boating, fishing, waterskiing, snow skiing, and working together for nearly 40 years.

During our career, I was the one pumping the gas, pushing us forward. You were the smart one with the intuition to know when to slow down or make a turn. It was that steady hand that accelerated our success.

Your social footprint was your paper business card, your handshake, and your word. It spread far and wide.

You were generous with your time, money, listening ability, and one-on-one "in the moment" conversations. When people were with you, they felt like they were the only person in the room. You always put everyone else first.

You lived from miracle to miracle. Your eyes were always wide open for the next exciting marvel to talk about. Whether it was the latest model Corvette or Super Yacht, the best hamburger, or the perfect piece of split oak to put on the fire. Your stories of these miracles always kept people waiting for the next word out of your mouth.

As you and Jeanne built your family, the values you embraced were sound, practical, loving, and kind. Family first, always! You have set the bar high for so many, and it shows in the love Elizabeth, Lucy, and Charlie have for you and Jeanne. The same holds true for my children, who have always admired you so much.

The life and relationship you and Jeanne created for each other is a model for others. Your deep love, compassion, care, and concern for each other were amazing. You both were admired and loved by so many.

Your service to others is not well-known except for the thousands you impacted. You never boasted or bragged. You just got it done in the quietest of caring ways. These people whose lives you altered are forever grateful for your help and guidance.

You leave huge holes in so many hearts. But for me, and I hope for others, I can learn to bring a piece of your soul into my body. You have always guided me in many aspects of my life, and I will continue to use your quiet internal judgment to help me make decisions.

Your departure was hard. Your body failed you in ways that are hard to talk about; ALS will do that. But all the while, your grace, dignity, and care for others were at the forefront of your daily practice. You never let us see your pain and suffering.

We had a great brotherhood with so many memorable moments. Laughing, crying, growing, failing, and then getting up and using those failures to become better.

Thank you for such a wonderful life together. You are in my soul, and I look forward to our chats.

God Bless you.

Rest in Peace, Brother Chuck

CHAPTER 24

SPIRITUALITY

When the topic of religion comes up in a conversation, especially when people start talking about how God and Jesus play a role in their lives, I always respond with my canned answer. "I am not very religious, but I am spiritual." As I'm writing this, I'm wondering, what does this really mean? Why do I always feel compelled to respond with this statement? Is it a defense mechanism? Do I not believe in God or that Jesus was the son of God?

As I am getting older, I have more and more questions I want answered about my faith.

This is another one of those topics in the book where there is no right or wrong way to believe. Our beliefs as they are today are formed by our exposure (or lack of exposure) to religious or spiritual communities. It can come from personal reflection, experiences of human loss and suffering, the healing from this suffering, and personal rituals and practices. I have friends that do not believe in God or any kind of higher power, and that's fine. This is another one of those very personal attributes of being a human. We can reason through anything and our beliefs are individual.

Having a strong faith system can be important on our journey. When you can lean in on a strong faith or the belief in a higher power, you might be able to find some meaning and purpose, or moral and ethical guidance. Many people use the belief in a higher power to cope with challenges through prayer, and also to find community. This is another area to be really curious about.

My story below and those of the men who responded to my questions cover a wide range of opinions and feelings. The most important part of this chapter is for you to locate and identify how you feel about spirituality. Ask some friends why they believe the way they do. Tell them you don't want to be convinced to join their belief, but rather want to understand what they believe and how they got there.

My story

I was brought up in a life of formal religion. The Mamaroneck Methodist Church on the Boston Post Road was our home. Every Sunday morning, we were at the 10:00 service. My sister, Susan, and brother, Chuck, were in the choir with me, so for many Sundays we sat with the adult choir for the first part of the service. But at 10:30, we were excused to head to Sunday school. My parents were both teachers and I remember them, on more than one occasion, complaining how hard this was to do with a hangover. I had yet to experience what a hangover was. All I knew was bad breath, bloodshot eyes, slow movements, cranky attitude, and how a bloody mary was a way for my dad to get energized.

I drifted away from the Church during college but reengaged after having children. I wanted my three sons to get exposure to religion. We found the Bedford Presbyterian Church in Bedford, New York and there began a 15-year relationship with that wonderful institution and community of people.

As I became more involved and led my children to the same experience I had as a child, I volunteered to help lead the youth group that had about 30 teenagers involved, including my three sons. Dr. Paul Alcorn (Paul) was the head pastor. We were contemporaries, and he had a passion for teaching religion through acts of service; especially for the youth of the

Church.

The youth group flourished, and my boys became good friends with many of the other kids their age and found their own way through religion. Monthly potluck dinners for the adults were a way in which we met so many new families who are still friends today. I felt a new connection to God as I spent more time with this community of people and through the service work we did.

The service work trips led by Paul were what really connected me to my spirituality. For five summers, we ventured to Hurley, Virginia to work with a local nonprofit making repairs to homes that otherwise had no way of getting fixed. In three 15-passenger vans, four adult leaders and 20–30 high school kids took the two-day journey. We spent five days doing a wide range of projects. Repairing porches and bathrooms that had rotted and fallen through the floor, and adding ramps so that a disabled person could get in and out easier. There were conversations at night where we reflected on giving back, helping others, having compassion, and so much more. Each trip deepened my spirituality and led me down a path of realizing my belief in a higher power existed, and it was service to others that nurtured my spirituality. My children still speak of those trips today.

We then became involved in week long trips to Nicaragua and the Dominican Republic as I reference in the chapter The Day My Heart Opened. On the first trip, we built two homes from the ground up for families living on the edge of survival. These new homes were constructed with concrete blocks, all reinforced with rebar to withstand hurricanes and earthquakes. We were in the village of Las Conchitas, a community of about 100 families. Most of them were living in tar paper shacks with dirt floors and have been living that way for generations.

This new 15'x15' concrete building had a raised tile floor, metal roof, windows, and doors, and felt like a mansion to the family. The physical and mental health of everyone living there improved dramatically.

At the end of the week, we all stood in a circle and blessed the home with the family. It was during these ceremonies that the love and gratitude from the family and community was overwhelming at times. In their words, they felt that God himself picked us up from our villages in New York, and delivered us to Nicaragua to do this work. All of us that day could feel the presence of God, or a higher power for some. I was so moved by this trip that I returned nearly 20 times over the following 15 years to bring others so that they could experience the same thing that I did.

It was my son Jonathan that encouraged me to join him on that first trip together and I am forever grateful to him asking me to go, as it changed the course of my faith. From that day forward, I had a better understanding of my spirituality, and that it was so much more than attending Church. It is now about living my life with all of the virtues I wrote about in this book. It is about believing in God and having a better understanding that prayer works. I find peace and happiness in prayer and feel it has the power to heal and help lead me on a path of serving others.

As you read the responses below, start thinking about your spiritual journey. You will have a chance to provide your own answers, but sit with these men and their answers and see what stirs your heart.

What do others have to say?

Here are some important questions with actual responses from other men like you:

Did you grow up with organized religion? Are you still involved? How has this influenced who you are today and the beliefs you have?

"My mom went to church on Christmas Eve sometimes. My father was an atheist. He said often that he wanted a question mark on his grave instead of the usual cross. He is buried (cremated) together with my mum (she died 27 years before him) and there is no question mark on the stone. I guess my sister and I were not brave enough to go against cultural norms and replace the cross with a question mark. I am also an atheist. I often discussed religion, nature, physics, the universe, and the big bang theory with my dad. We found common understanding (and both enjoyed the writings of Stephen Hawking) and we both agreed that there is no God in the sense of what religion in our part of the world maintained. Religion contains social norms and many other things that are useful for a society. But I believe there is no God that has created us, or anything else for that matter."

Rolf J.

"I grew up in an organized religion. I was baptized into the Roman Catholic Church very early in my life. I attended Catholic elementary, high school, college and grad school. I was an Altar Boy in my youth. Yes, I'm still involved, attending Mass at my local parish in Pleasantville, New York, most Sundays and have been known to 'drop in' to Catholic churches during the week as I serve my clients in the Greater New York area or travel around the country. My faith has had a significant influence on my beliefs throughout my life. It has provided structure and an underlying basis in terms of my day to day activities."

Matthew M.

"Today I still attend church regularly, but have become more prayerful in recent years. I believe my faith defines me more today than the church I attend. That said, I hold most of the Catholic faith teachings very close to my heart. My wife is Presbyterian. We were married in her church. Our daughters were baptized and raised Presbyterian. I was an active participant in their faith journeys. Having spent 40 years in a multi-faith marriage, I am so much better a person. Much more rounded in my faith and a greater appreciation for others' church, faith."

Anonymous

Religion is usually a set of organized beliefs and practices shared by a community. Spirituality is more of an individual practice and has to do with having a sense of peace and purpose. What gives your life meaning and leaves you feeling purposeful?

"Making an impact. If things I do result in a measurable improved outcome, I feel good. I know that what I did had an impact. That gives my life purpose."

James W.

"I am not religious and I don't think of myself as spiritual, yet I derive tremendous meaning from a variety of daily acts. I have drawn inspiration from so many others—from survivors of the Holocaust who went on to lead positive lives of helping others, to hundreds of examples of volunteer leaders who put their self-interest aside to help others. I derive meaning from honoring the acts of others and helping others. I feel purposeful in helping others. That gives me satisfaction."

Chuck N.

"This is such a challenging question because I think the two are way more intertwined than most people discuss. I have gained spirituality through religion and have sought religion through spirituality in many cases. As a Christian, I believe what is taught. I believe in the power of Jesus. I feel Jesus gives my life purpose, hope, and grace, and the challenge to live as Christlike as possible. Jesus came to love, serve, and forgive, and he also came to teach truth. This is such a difficult line, but it provides me with both meaning and purpose. I think we often lose sight of the wonders of this earth and the wonders of every single human being."

Brent K.

What do you think happens when we die?

"When we die I think our soul goes somewhere. As I watched my mother die, she could clearly see the 'other side' where she saw my father and others she loved. She talked to them and told me about them. That experience solidified my belief that there is a place where we will be reunited with loved ones. It is commonly known as heaven. It certainly exists for me. Religion gives us a roadmap showing how to get there. Not sure I agree with all aspects of their map, but I think that's where I will go."

Anonymous

"I have no idea what happens when we die. If I am to be honest, I think you are gone. What isn't gone however is your legacy and your lessons. They live on in your children and are passed forward to their children."

Anonymous

"I think there is an afterlife. Hard to know what shape or form, but I do believe everyone's soul lives on."

Mark K.

"I believe in life after death, the immortality of the soul, and the physical resurrection of the body at a time in the future. In my opinion, it is important to live a good life so that our creator will reward me in my afterlife."

Charles W.

Any other thoughts on spirituality?

"I miss the 'fellowship,' the sense of belonging to a community that I felt as a kid. Also the certainty. We were so certain. That's what we were taught. Today, questions have taken over."

Anonymous

"As much as I have a lover's quarrel with church and organized religion, it is the one place where I hear words like grace, and justice, and stewardship, and responsibility, and inclusion spoken out loud. Somehow, hearing those words reminds me of core values in my life, and the more I honor those values the more balanced and better off I am."

Paul A.

"I think we humans are more than the sum of our individual selves. That we are greater as a whole than we are as individual humans. Perhaps 'spirituality' outside of a religious context is recognizing that living in ways that benefit others is more than repaid to our own individual benefit, that contributing to the whole of us collectively should be our shared purpose. Imagine if everyone lived by that thought!"

Ken F.

"I wish I had a more significant purpose in my life, in my relationships, in my future, but I just don't, and that bothers me. Maybe more religion and spirituality in my life would give me more purpose. I'm not sure."

Anonymous

Your Turn:

If you want the best results possible from this book, answer the journaling questions before moving onto the next section.

Did you grow up with organized religion? Are you still involved? How has this influenced who you are today and the beliefs you have?

_____

_____

_____

_____

_____

Religion is usually a set of organized beliefs and practices shared by a community. Spirituality is more of an individual practice and has to do with having a sense of peace and purpose. What gives your life meaning and leaves you feeling purposeful?

_____

_____

_____

_____

_____

What do you think happens when we die?

_____

_____

_____

_____

Any other thoughts on spirituality?

_____

_____

_____

My challenge to you

Now that you have given this topic some thought, here is my challenge to you:

Now that you have completed the journaling questions above, you have a pretty good idea of your current beliefs. But you also may have some questions you want answered and have some more learning to do in this area.

If that is the case then here are some suggestions I have for you.

Find a friend or two to discuss these ideas and concepts of religion, spirituality, God, a higher power, heaven, hell, dying, and more. In Chapter Ten we talked a lot about curiosity and learning. I want you to apply that thinking to this topic.

Since this might not be the topic that you normally chat about with close friends, open the door to trying it. Have an open mind, don't be defensive about your beliefs as much as curious about your friends' beliefs. And don't judge or criticize what your friends' beliefs are.

Here are some questions you can use for this conversation with your friends and, frankly, a conversation with your partner, children, or siblings.

- ☐ Do you believe in God? What or why not? How is that belief serving you?
- ☐ If you do not believe in God, do you believe in a higher power? What or who is that power?
- ☐ Do you pray at all, and what does that look like for you? Do you feel like your prayers are being answered? How does your praying help you?
- ☐ Do you belong to a spiritual or religious community? If so, why, and what does it do for you?
- ☐ Do you have any memory of a time in your life that you had a deep spiritual awakening or experience?
- ☐ Do you feel like this is a part of your life that you have ignored and want to understand more?

Have you ever faced doubts or had challenges in your life that led you to lean in on your spirituality? How did you overcome these challenges?

I hope that these questions stir something inside of you that lead you to some answers and deeper thinking on this topic.

CHAPTER 25

LEGACY

This is the final chapter where I guide you with a story and then a challenge on how to implement what you have learned. Everything you have worked on up to this point will become part of your legacy. It is part of it now, and it's up to you to determine if that legacy is what you want to leave behind or if it needs some work.

Think of your legacy as the blueprint of your life; the guiding principles that drive your behavior, your morals, and your core values. This book is meant to give you a path to learn more about yourself and then implement changes to evolve into a better man. Use all that you have learned so far and create an action plan to become the kind of person you want to be remembered as.

Jody calls our lives the dash in our tombstone. From the day we are born until the day we die, we are creating a legacy. I have given a lot of thought to my legacy as a result of this conversation with Jody. As I age and see that my window of time here is closing, it's becoming more important to do as much as I can to leave the world better than when I arrived. If I can accomplish that, then I feel like I had a well-lived life.

Your legacy is what you leave behind for others to remember you by. Your beliefs, your values, your traditions, and more. It can be financial as well, leaving something behind for your heirs.

I think that it's important to think more about this so that, before you do depart, you put some thought into what you would like people to say at your funeral. What kind of man was I? Was I a good parent, a good husband, a good leader? These questions and more can help shape who we are going forward. This book is about self-reflection in the areas of your life that can all impact your legacy.

When you read the letter I wrote to myself from my future 90-year-old self, know that was a start for me to think about how I want to be remembered. I have changed how I live my life, and a big part of that change has been to serve others in a way that I am making their lives better. This applies to Jody, my six children, their partners, my grandchildren, friends, and other family. Part of my legacy is this book (and hopefully more books) as well as the business Jody and I created to help people flourish in retirement.

When I retired from my career in 2018, I had created a wonderful legacy. I was 61 years old and spent 38 years building several businesses, I created a wonderful family, and had a stellar career that included serving on a dozen non-profit boards. If I had died then, I knew my obituary would be full of all my great business accomplishments, my life as a family man, and my work in the nonprofit community. But what if I live 30 more years? All of that would be old news. I realized there was more that I could do.

What is your legacy? Have you given the right amount of thought to this topic?

My story

My dad lived a full life up until 65 when he retired. At that point, he chose the route of sitting back, taking it easy, and "enjoying the fruits of his labor," as he used to say. He was a loving father, husband, and family man. He grew the family business and sold it to me and my brother as fourth generation owners. He was active in Rotary International and other non-profit organizations, giving of his time, talents, and financial resources. He was well-liked and respected in the business community. But I think he could have done more.

When he sold the business to us and stepped away from his role as CEO of our family business, his involvement in giving back ended. He took all his God-given talents, his connections in the business community, all his experiences, knowledge, and wisdom, and put it in a box, tied it up with a nice bow, and put it on the shelf in the garage. That was his choice, and frankly it was not a good one in my opinion. With all his newfound time in retirement, he lost his way because he did not have anything to work on, anything to share with others, anything to create with his skills and talents.

In my mind, my father failed at retirement. He lost his way on his self-care, his relationships, his ability to forgive, and he held onto regrets until the day he died. As I watched him during his last 15 years of life—his retirement phase—I was motivated not to take the same path.

Jody and I have taken a different path. We feel like our lives are just beginning. Everything we have done up until now has been preparations for this third phase of life. And we have already done a lot. When we retired in December 2018, our lives were full. If we had to write our obituaries back then, they would be complete. All good things, and a great legacy for others to talk about and admire. But given the fact that we believe we will live to 100, we have what feels like a lifetime left to fill. If we do live to 100, and do nothing more to make a difference, all of what we accomplished up to 2018 would be very old news.

We knew we wanted to live a long healthy retirement. At 66, I still have 24 years until I am 90, at which point I may slow down a bit, but I don't know. What I do know is that I am not sitting on my laurels, sliding through this time in life. We have worked hard for five years, building a retirement life for ourselves, focusing on our five pillars: physical and mental wellness, relationships, spouse-partner relationships, and finally wisdom sharing. With these pillars, we tap into our knowledge, skills, and experience to coach and mentor young adults to help them with their careers.

We want to continue to support, encourage, build, love, and nurture our six children, their partners, and their children. It's critically important to us to be in their lives in a way that they feel connected to us, tap into our wisdom and experiences to fast track their lives, and come to us for opinions, advice, help when in trouble, and unconditional love. This is not always easy. Personalities can get in the way. We must be careful to not overdo our advice. We have seen already that our children are going to parent differently than us. We cannot expect them to behave exactly as we think they should, so giving out advice and counsel needs to be done carefully.

We want them to remember us as kind, non-judgmental, helpful parents and grandparents that were always there to provide a helping hand. We have friends that have children who are estranged. Something happened to push them away. We all are capable of making mistakes and hurting each other, but now is the time to work through that.

As we age, we need to keep these close meaningful relationships alive and nurture them. As social animals, we need strong solid, meaningful relationships with people to ward off loneliness, depression and, frankly, suicide.

What do others have to say?

Here are some important questions with actual responses from other men like you:

How important is your legacy to you and why? Think of family, friends, your business and finances, and the community at large.

"I really have not given this much thought until I read your question. I think that if my family, friends, and business associates remember me as someone they could always count on to help them in their daily lives (not necessarily financially), that would be good enough for me."

Anonymous

"When I think of 'legacy,' I think of what others might think when they think of me after I'm gone. It is somewhat like a post-mortem brand, and we all know how important a 'brand' is. Having said that, I don't need my name on a building or a park bench, I just want those that I love and those that I worked with to have a positive memory of my time on earth."

Jeffrey C.

Who would you want to speak at your funeral and what would you want them to say about you?

"I would like my brothers, my priest, and my wife to speak. I would like them to say that I was a kind caring person who was fair and thoughtful of others, and I was always willing to give of myself in time, talent, and money."

Mark K.

"At my funeral or memorial service, I hope whoever speaks would focus more on who I was than on what I did. That I was kind. That I cared. That, with all my mistakes and flaws, I did my best to be a good husband and father and grandfather and friend. That I cared about the communities in which I lived and the 'neighbors' who were a part of my life. I hope my kids will be the ones who speak."

Paul A.

"My daughter and son. I hope they will say that I lived a good life, and they learned some great experiences and life lessons that have helped them in their lives with their families."

Keith D.

What are some things you can do differently today to build a legacy you would be proud of?

"Take more time to listen carefully to those around me."

James W.

"I think I could be more involved in community activities, such as Habitat for Humanity or the like. Doing so may not exactly build on my legacy, but there is a need and I should get more involved."

David C.

"Possibly slow down a bit and enjoy the moment. Time passes quickly and spending quality time with family and friends builds a foundation for a happy life. Maybe be a more open communicator and don't hold things inside."

Keith D.

Any other thoughts on legacy?

"Your legacy will eventually be determined by others, so being the best human you can be is much more important than trying to create a legacy."

Joseph A.

"They say a brand is what people say about you when you are not present. I think legacy is much the same. I want to leave the world a better place than how I found it."

Brent K.

"I have done hundreds of funerals. No one gives a shit about worldly accomplishments. They don't want to hear it. They want to know how the person's character lives on."

Carter V.

Your Turn:

If you want the best results possible from this book, answer the journaling questions before moving onto the next section.

How important is your legacy to you and why? Think of family, friends, your business and finances, and the community at large.

_____
_____
_____
_____
_____

Who would you want to speak at your funeral and what would you want them to say about you?

_____
_____
_____
_____
_____

What are some things you can do differently today to build a legacy you would be proud of?

_____
_____
_____
_____
_____

Any other thoughts on grieving or legacy?

_____
_____
_____

My challenge to you

Now that you have given this topic some thought, here is my challenge to you:

To expand more on the idea of that dash in your tombstone, Jody tells this great story about how it represents everything you did from birth until your death. This dash could fill volumes of books, but it's the executive summary that matters. The difference you made to peoples' lives. The legacy you leave behind.

I want you to write a letter to yourself from your future 90-year-old self. The letter I wrote to myself is in the next chapter, for your inspiration. You can read it now, or work on your own letter first.

Part of this exercise for me was to manifest all that I want to become and accomplish over the next 25 years. I want you to make this fun. Really use your imagination to see yourself at the age of 90. What you look like, where you are living, who your closest friends are, and all the goodness you have in your heart after living for 90 years.

Framework for writing a letter from your 90-year-old self

Get out a journal or laptop and start writing using the following framework. Don't think too hard about what you write; I want you to feel it from your heart and not your brain. If you think too hard about it, the words may not flow. And this can be a living document that you go back to on occasion and edit. I read mine at least once a month when I'm feeling down, sad, or wondering what I want to do with the rest of my life.

Don't try and do it all in one sitting, but stretch this out over a few weeks or a month. Make sure you are in the right mood for this project. Get your favorite drink, find your favorite place, and do it when your mind is most clear and creative. For me that is always early in the morning.

Start with the date of your 90th birthday, and address it "Dear, [your name]." And then, start writing, thinking about these categories:

Date & setting

Close your eyes for a minute and visualize yourself in a setting in your home, perhaps having your favorite drink in your favorite room.

- ☐ What is the date?
- ☐ What are your plans for the day?
- ☐ What are your primary emotions that day?
- ☐ Where are you sitting and what is the atmosphere like?

Retrospection

- ☐ Reflect on the key moments that triggered significant changes in your life, such as retirement, a second career, the birth of a child or loss of a family member, or other life-changing moments.
- ☐ Also make note of some past indiscretions that you may be holding on to as regrets. Reframe them as lessons learned. Accept the fact that you are human and make mistakes, and that you have flaws. But from this day forward, you are working on being a better human.
- ☐ Who are some key relationships that helped you get where you are at 90?
- ☐ Who stood by you? How have those relationships evolved? Which friends will be with you on your 90th birthday?
- ☐ Who in your family will be with you on your 90th birthday and what will they say to you?

Pivotal achievements

- ☐ Make a list of all the significant milestones and achievements from today forward, professionally and personally.
- ☐ How did your past actions set you up for the next number of years until your 90th birthday?
- ☐ How did you surprise yourself, and others, with all that you did since today?
- ☐ In what way did you exceed everyone's expectations?

Professional & personal evolution

- ☐ If you are still working, or plan on a second or third career as you age, highlight all of the ventures, projects, books, good business moves, or other significant things you have completed.
- ☐ What is primarily different about you as a person at 90 than you as you are today?
- ☐ What are some major personal growth achievements you are proud of?

Health & wellness

- What is your vision today for your health and wellness at the age of 90? Reiterate how you were able to achieve that vision.
- What are some of the things you did to make that vision a reality?
- Mention some of the bad habits you eliminated and new healthy habits you incorporated into your life that helped get you to 90.
- What are some challenges you overcame to achieve your vision?

Legacy & impact

- Reflect on your legacy of today, then add to it what has changed now that you are 90.
- Who have you inspired along the way? Family, friends, a specific population, or the community at large?
- Who around you is carrying on with some initiatives you may have started?

Current state & gratitude

- Talk about your present situation, feelings, and the individuals around you.
- Write about some deep gratitude towards your younger self for setting the foundation and to others who have played a pivotal role in your life.

Closing thoughts & a glimpse into the future

- What are your current aspirations or beliefs about the future? Even at 90, what are you looking forward to?
- Close the letter with a heartfelt thank you to your past-self for starting this journey and creating a lasting legacy.

This is meant to be a fun, exciting, and joyful exercise. Make sure you have a smile on your face and an open heart as you write this letter.

And if you are comfortable please send me a copy. I would love to read it.

Send it to mrollins@markhamrollins.com

CHAPTER 26

LETTER FROM MY 90-YEAR-OLD SELF

April 15, 2047

Dear Markham,

As I sit here on my 90th birthday, I can't help but reflect on September 29th, 2022, when you asked me to write this letter.

My life is filled with love, kindness, fulfillment and more. My relationship with Jody is better than ever before. My children and grandchildren all look to me for sage advice and a dose of wisdom when they need it. My health is exactly what your vision predicted back in 2022. I am physically independent, fully aware mentally of my surroundings, and living deep personal relationships with family and friends.

None of this would have been possible for me at 90 if you did not have the courage, passion, drive, and discipline to make all the changes you made 25 years ago. To this day, I still rise early, exercise, meditate, journal, and share morning coffee with Jody. I am forever grateful for all that you did to get me here. Thank you from the bottom of my heart.

At 65, your life was complete. You helped raise six children. You had a successful career as a fourth-generation business owner, and you made all the right financial decisions so that you were financially independent at the age of 65. You always told people back then that if your death came early, you were okay. You felt you had achieved so much that you would be okay. You felt that your loved ones would miss you, but you were confident you did all the things necessary to launch them successfully into the world. And your funeral would be full, and your legacy intact.

You surprised everyone with your next 25 years. Your legacy up to 65 is just a footnote to the legacy you leave behind now. And I want to thank you for everything you did to get me where I am today.

When you attempted retirement and realized you were in trouble, you and Jody quickly made changes to your life. Your idea to start Retirement Transformed to help others also thrive in this third phase of life has really caught on. You were early in the game of changing how future generations spend their time in retirement. As a matter of fact, people don't even use that word anymore. High schools and colleges, as well as companies, provide tools to let people reimagine this phase of their future lives. No longer do their ads show people sitting on beaches with piña coladas.

Your first book was a launch pad for such greater work in this area, teaching men to be more in touch with their inner-self and to embrace the core values and beliefs that can guide them. You gave them a road map on how to make the changes needed to be better human beings.

All your books have made an impact on people's lives. Your speeches still command a standing ovation, and you have created a movement for men who want to evolve.

Your vision for wellness, of being "physically independent at the age of 90," is ringing so loud today. All those times you *almost* did not exercise at 5:00 a.m., or when you *almost* ate the whole bag of Oreos, or *almost* drank too much alcohol at dinners, all contributed to my lasting health today.

While the years have flown by, there are so many unique and special moments that I can recall, and I am grateful for all of them. I think back to the first book, *The Evolving Man: Life Virtues Men Don't Talk About* and

I'm so grateful that you wrote it. It was a launch pad for who I am today. You helped countless other men and women learn to be better humans and to build lasting relationships, and helped them thrive in life.

Before you wrote your first book, you were a good man. But the process of writing the book was a launchpad for you personally, and I am so grateful for who I evolved into today. Your understanding of what it means to live a life of humility has served me well and I still work on this important area of my life. And to this day, I continue to work on my listening skills, always trying to be in the moment during conversations.

I love how you set me on a path of forgiveness, including forgiving yourself to be able to move forward with a clean slate. And you became vulnerable to the point that you were always honest, sincere, direct, and not afraid of having difficult conversations. Your compassion and empathy were shining examples for others, and I am proud of you.

The way in which you created and nurtured relationships became the gold standard for others. And my marriage to Jody was always growing, getting deeper, and becoming stronger to the point we almost act as one today.

As I sit here today, I am grateful for the way in which I look at my own death and the spiritual beliefs I now have due to your hard work. My legacy is intact and filled with more than I imagined back at age 65. But you set the table for me. And not only did I learn, but I also taught others everything I learned.

I am at peace, and I still believe I will live to be 100 or more. But now, I rest. I still have a few clients that I help, but I'm more focused on my children, Jody, and our grandchildren. We still have at least one time a year where we all gather.

Thank you again for starting what you started. For not quitting, and for having the vision and drive to help men evolve and to make Retirement Transformed into a global movement.

With Love,

Markham
Your future 90-year-old self

SECTION 4
MY FINAL CHALLENGE TO YOU

CHAPTER 27

WHAT'S NEXT FOR YOU?

Congratulations on all the hard work you put into your life while reading this book! No matter how much work you did, you are different now. I know you can feel it, and I know you feel better about who you have become.

You have woken up to your new life. You notice it, and the people in your life notice it.

When you look back on all the life virtue chapters, these words now mean something to you. You listened to what I had to say, and also to the other men that participated in the journaling. And you sat, opened your heart, and pulled on your emotions to write your own answers to the journaling questions.

You read the challenges I gave to you and made yourself think deeper about what you can do to be a better father, husband, son, friend and overall human being.

You have learned to be a better listener, and opened your heart to being more vulnerable.

Look back at your notes and the work you did:

- ☐ You are now a better **listener** and can sit in conversations with **kindness**, **empathy** and **curiosity**. You don't rush to answer, but truly listen.
- ☐ The openness you now have to **forgive** yourself and others has lightened the load on your mind.
- ☐ **Regrets** now look more like life lessons than burdens you carry around of mistakes that cannot be undone.
- ☐ Your ability to be **vulnerable** with those that you love has deepened those **relationships** and brought you a new level of happiness.
- ☐ You have worked on your **ego** and **humility,** and people are noticing the positive change in you. Embrace that change and keep working on this.
- ☐ You are thinking hard about how you process **grief** and also your **spiritual journey**. Don't stop with this processing. These are both important as we begin to lose loved ones and question our faith.
- ☐ You have learned to **love** yourself and others, and let your heart help lead you to always do the next right thing.
- ☐ With all of the above, and especially the opening of your heart, you have become more **grateful**. Instead of wanting more, you are grateful for what you have.
- ☐ You have committed to a program of **self-care** and made this a priority in your life.
- ☐ **Sex and intimacy** are now part of your **marriage** or primary relationship. This is a big area for all of us and you are committed to work on it.
- ☐ Your **legacy** is now on your mind and can be the driver for everything you have learned reading this book. How you are remembered is critically important to you now. The letter you wrote from your 90-year-old self will manifest itself in your daily behaviors.

You cannot end this book by going back to sleep. You cannot go back to who you were with your old ways. That's easy to do and comfortable for you. But you can't let that happen.

Here is my overall challenge to you:

- ☐ Keep a journal and make writing part of your daily routine. Even a few words, but sit and reflect on your life and day.
- ☐ Download the workbook and do the work.
- ☐ Once you do the work—specifically the challenges—document your journey. Go back and reread what you wrote so that it begins to become your new normal.

Thank you for joining me on our journey of evolving. It will never end for us. We will continue to work on being better versions of ourselves for the rest of our lives.

The world needs more evolved men like you and me to set the example for others. You owe this change to yourself and also those around you. If you have children, especially sons, then you must share this with them. Talk about some of these virtues and how they can become better men and humans.

And finally, please send me an email with your thoughts and make sure you subscribe and stay tuned for future books and materials to further this journey.

mrollins@markhamrollins.com

I'm so grateful to be part of your life and that you are now part of mine.

www.ingramcontent.com/pod-product-compliance
Lightning Source LLC
Chambersburg PA
CBHW050252010526
44107CB00003B/295